time to read

Examples of Reader Development Work from North West libraries 2001 – 2004

A good practice guide produced by the North West library network **Time to Read**

Contents

Editorial

I am delighted to have had the opportunity to edit this publication, which is a celebration of reader development work in libraries in the North West of England.

It follows up a publication that I put together for The National Year of Reading in 1998 which provided a snapshot of projects and promotions in the region at that time. There was very little co-operation between authorities and most work was being done on a shoestring.

The picture is very different six years on. DCMS Wolfson funded projects have made a big impact in the North West, the network has grown from strength to strength and levered in funding to support reader development work across authorities. Endorsement and support now comes from the highest levels of library planning:

Libraries do not just provide a store of books: they help people experience and enjoy the pleasure of reading. In recent years there has been an important shift in how libraries view and plan their work with reading. As well as its importance as a tool for learning, they have recognised its creative, imaginative role in people's lives.
Framework for the Future – Libraries, Learning and Information in the Next Decade
4.7 p25.

The picture nationally is much more co-ordinated, following on from the large scale training programme, *Branching Out*, co-ordinated by Opening the Book, which encouraged sharing of skills across the country. Libraries now gain access to major media promotions such as The BBC's *Big Read*, and The Reading Agency's Summer Reading promotions that support work with young people.

Libraries' approach to reader development is becoming increasingly sophisticated. Library authorities are working together to create new structures enabling programmes to be delivered both regionally and nationally.
Framework for the Future 4.8 p26

There is still a large amount of work to be done to spread these benefits and ensure that reader development becomes embedded in the strategies of the future. This book shows the innovation, progress and excitement demonstrated by those working in the field.

Anne Caldwell
Freelance writer and Literature Development Consultant

A Co-ordinator's Perspective

I have been proud to co-ordinate the Time To Read network (TTR) since October 2002. As a founder member of a small team brought together through a pioneering Opening the Book training course in 1996, I have been able to contribute to the development of the Network to the exciting point it is at now, with all 22 authorities in the region involved.

The Arts Council England NW has always supported generously, placing libraries and reader development at the core of the cultural agenda in the region. This year (2004) a new partnership with MLA North West has developed. Their support will open up new opportunities and ensure that reader development is a key part of the public libraries' agenda in this region. Partnership with Libraries NW means that TTR is brought into closer contact with other library sectors in the region. The Society of Chief Librarians NW has recently strengthened support and will be playing a firmer role in steering network activities.

So TTR has grown from a grassroots network of reader development activists into being a strategic force in the region. The Public Libraries Challenge Fund (PLCF) provided the chance to show what we could do. TTR had already demonstrated that authorities across the region were willing and able to co-operate on a large-scale joint project. Julie Spencer (Bolton Libraries) who co-ordinated the *Reading Lifelines* and *Everybody's Reading* projects, successfully pioneered the role of regional co-ordinator and developed the model for building a cross-authority team.

Of course development in this region hasn't happened in isolation from the rest of the country. Through the PLCF, library services nationally proved the value of investing in reader development. The Reading Agency and Opening the Book both now continue to open up new opportunities, forge new national partnerships and act as passionate advocates for books, reading and innovative projects. *Framework for the Future* has books and reading at its heart and provides the strongest reason currently for increased focus on reading activity.

The role of regional co-ordinator exists to work at the strategic level, providing advocacy and looking for new partnership and funding opportunities. I can provide a direct link to national project managers, co-ordinating responses and feedback. The key role is still to provide practical support to reader development practitioners in the region. By sharing ideas and best practice, organising training and regular network meetings, and by producing materials and activities that can be used 'at the front line' I aim to enhance the range of activity and enthuse and energise continuous good practice across the region.

The co-ordinator post is now funded until Sept 2006. I would like to take this opportunity to thank all members of the network in the region, and their chief officers, for giving me the opportunity to work on their behalf in an area of work I am passionate about. I would particularly like to thank Manchester Library and Information Service for giving me the opportunity to continue in this role and for providing enhanced support for the Time To Read network.

Jane Mathieson
Time to Read Co-ordinator

Continuing Support from the Arts Council England, North West

Just a week before Jane Mathieson, co-ordinator of the North West region's Time To Read consortium, asked me to write an introduction for this publication, a pamphlet dropped onto my desk that had been produced by Demos, the government think tank, and funded by The Reading Agency, the national Arts Council funded agency for the promotion of reader development. The pamphlet was about 'Creative Reading' for young people, reading and public libraries. I was delighted to see the publication if only because it recognised that the ideas we have all been working towards for the last ten or so years have finally established themselves at an influential level.

Looking back on the 1998 publication *Time To Promote Reading,* funded by the then North West Arts Board, it is remarkable to see how things have moved on. Now in the North West region there are 22 library authorities prepared to sign up to supporting the ongoing work of the Time To Read consortium alongside Arts Council funding – then there were many fewer.

In 2004 reader development is built into the libraries' *Framework for the Future* document, which means that the work of a hands-on agency such as Time To Read is finally pushing at open doors, at all sorts of levels within libraries and beyond.

Despite the geographical and population size of the North West and the inevitable teething troubles in establishing such an agency, from consultancy recommendations, through to levering commitment and funding, we are now in a situation where most library authorities have a dedicated librarian or team with reader development responsibility. Time To Read, from its early project-based beginnings, has grown into an organisation that supports these staff and deals directly with libraries' needs. The organisation now is in a position to speak more widely about its successes. This publication will showcase a wide range of projects, models and strategies that have been drawn directly from library experience here in our diverse and vibrant region.

The new Comprehensive Spending Review with its focus on museums and libraries will allow the literature remit of the Arts Council to continue to be delivered, with the support of the new NW Literature Officer. Reading is firmly placed within the local authority Arts Council agenda by libraries, and Time To Read is growing into an established agency that can deliver a strategic business plan already developed by its members and led by Jane Mathieson, Time To Read's co-ordinator.

A vision for the future? A network of libraries intimately linked with the literature networks regionally and nationally, and particularly with our national and regional small presses, independent publishers and literary magazines - bringing new writing to north west readers – and doing it day by day in the way that Time To Read and its partner library authorities have done so well so far.

Bronwen Williams
Literature Officer
Arts Council England, North West

New Partner, Museums, Libraries & Archives

MLA North West is a new organisation since the last edition of this publication. We aim to be the organisation connecting "people to knowledge and information, creativity and inspiration." (MLA Mission Statement 2004)

We count ourselves fortunate to be working in a region with an existing strong, grass-roots reader development organisation such as Time To Read, with an established track record of sharing best practice in this field.

So how can MLA North West contribute?

· First of all, advocacy. We are celebrating the success of Time To Read as an exemplar of regional working by taking every opportunity to highlight the project to other agencies in the North West and at national level. Not only does this promote the project, but also the value of libraries to culture, the arts, learning and social inclusion.

· We are working practically with Time To Read on a variety of wider development projects. For example, helping libraries to use the *Inspiring Learning for All* framework to enhance their reader development activities. This helps to mainstream reader development into the wider change agenda for libraries.

· Last, but not least, we have developed a close and supportive ongoing relationship for the future.

We look forward to assisting with the development of a new three year strategy for reader development, and helping bring the joy and value of reading to even more people, wherever they live, across the North West.

Alan Boughey
Libraries Development Officer

MLA North West
Malt Building, Wilderspool Park,
Greenalls Avenue, Warrington, WA4 6HL
Tel. 01925-625063
www.mlanorthwest.org.uk

Photo: Ian Lawson. Blackburn Station
www.englandsnorthwest.com/

One of the many questions I am asked as a reader development specialist is how to sustain work in this field over a period of time. Often the answer comes down to money.

The North West of England benefited from two long-term reader development projects funded through DCMS Public Libraries Challenge Fund between the years 2000 and 2002. *Reading Lifelines* and *Everybody's Reading* were co-ordinated by Time to Read who employed Julie Spencer from Bolton Libraries to oversee the projects. Both were aimed at 16-25 year olds who were living in the North West and experiencing social exclusion. These ground breaking projects were the first time that a large number of authorities had worked together and have set a pattern for a more co-operative way of working and sharing resources. In the first project, outreach workers were employed, or computer hardware purchased to improve library facilities for the target group. Much of the project involved making new contacts in the communities of the North West and engaging young people in reading activities.

During *Everybody's Reading*, eighteen part-time project outreach workers, a co-ordinator and a webmaster worked on the project using arts-based approaches; youth work techniques, a large scale promotional campaign and a website to engage young people into the library service. The projects finished with a national conference that showcased the good practice and brought people from all over the country to share experience in this field. While some of the work from these schemes was able to be built into the mainstream practices of library work, other authorities struggled to continue projects beyond their funding period.

Anne Caldwell

Halton Daemons Wargaming Club
Halton Borough Council October 2002 – present
Targeting boys 12-18years

Description of Project

In 2002, as part of the *Everybody's Reading* project, Halton Libraries teamed up with Games Workshop to stage two *Lord of the Rings* events. At that time the interest in *The Lord of the Rings*, due to the film, was immense and there was awareness of the popularity of Games Workshop amongst the target age group.

Both events were heavily over-subscribed and the majority of the tickets were distributed within the first few days of the events being promoted.

The Halton Daemons now meet every two weeks in the library. We have over 165 members (they don't all come every week, thank goodness!). The ages of the members are predominantly 12-18 year olds and include lads and dads, girls and even a mum. The atmosphere is fantastic and it's great to see the older members (who we have delegated as mentors) welcoming and encouraging new and/or younger members.

We run the club as a community club, thus allowing us to access various funding that is available to us. We have received four amounts of funding: one from the Arts Council, three from local sources. This has allowed us to hold a range of events, some taking place over a week, which has attracted more members.

It is rare that you get an initiative in this area that actually works and brings so many young people into the library on a regular basis. The club combines elements of reader development, creative writing, teamwork skills, art development and increased library membership.

Our methodology is featured on the Literacy Trust website as part of their *Lord of the Rings in Libraries* report:
http://www.readon.org.uk/campaign/bookedup/Report.pdf
and our Halton Daemons website is at: www.halton-daemons.co.uk

Feedback from members

It was boss! It was class! It was cool!

I think events like this with the Games Workshop are an excellent idea, bringing kids into the library as a place of community spirit

Tips for other authorities wishing to repeat idea

• Approach your local Games Workshop for help and advice.

• Start with small one-off events to gauge local interest.

• Promote, promote, promote!

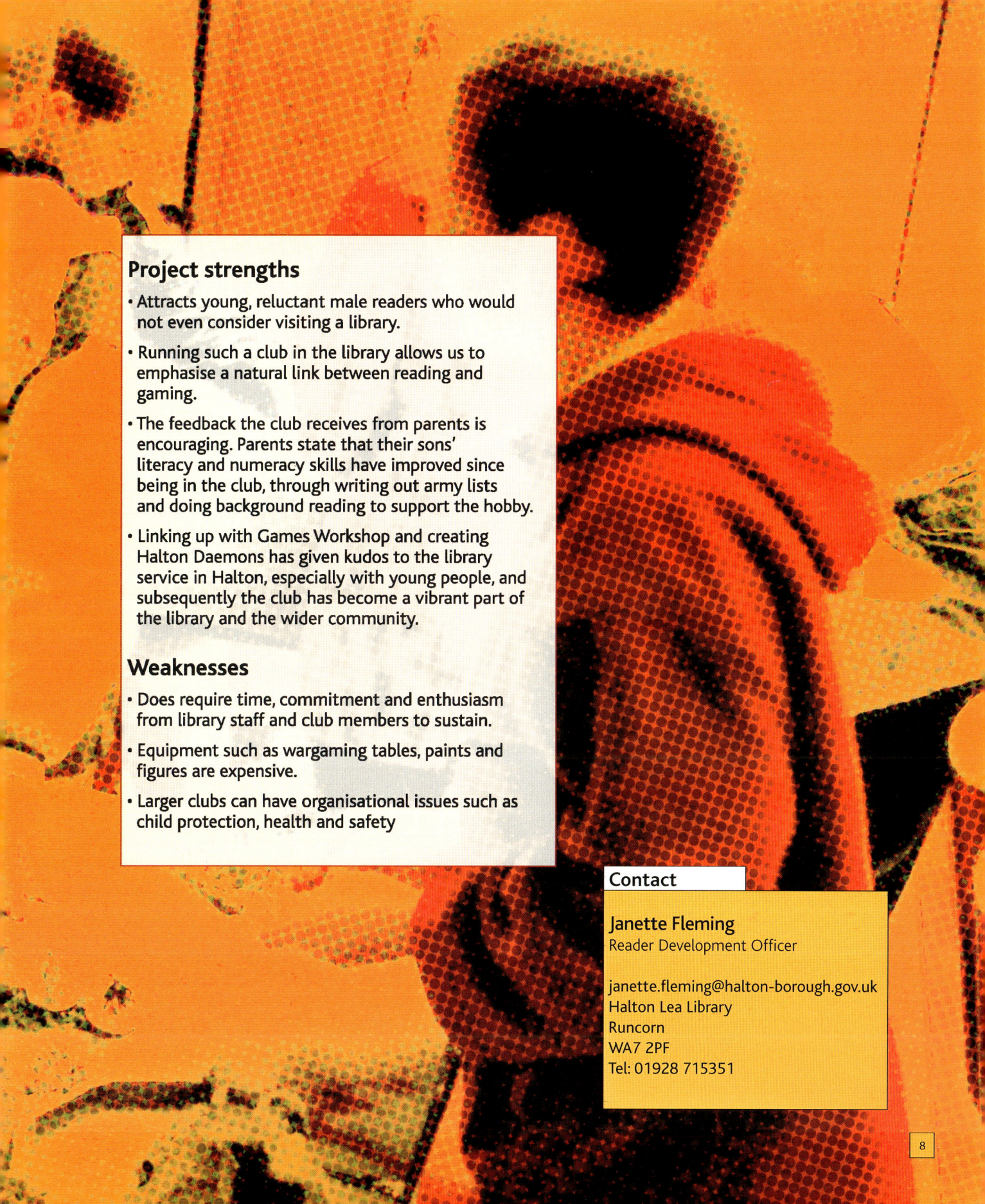

Project strengths

- Attracts young, reluctant male readers who would not even consider visiting a library.

- Running such a club in the library allows us to emphasise a natural link between reading and gaming.

- The feedback the club receives from parents is encouraging. Parents state that their sons' literacy and numeracy skills have improved since being in the club, through writing out army lists and doing background reading to support the hobby.

- Linking up with Games Workshop and creating Halton Daemons has given kudos to the library service in Halton, especially with young people, and subsequently the club has become a vibrant part of the library and the wider community.

Weaknesses

- Does require time, commitment and enthusiasm from library staff and club members to sustain.

- Equipment such as wargaming tables, paints and figures are expensive.

- Larger clubs can have organisational issues such as child protection, health and safety

Contact

Janette Fleming
Reader Development Officer

janette.fleming@halton-borough.gov.uk
Halton Lea Library
Runcorn
WA7 2PF
Tel: 01928 715351

Description of Project

Outreach worker Paula Tighe was employed in Oldham to co-ordinate the *Everybody's Reading* project locally. She worked at Broadway and Fitton Hill Libraries in the Borough organising young events and workshops that tied into Oldham's *Festival of Words* and Black History Month celebrations. In June 2001, a more strategic approach was adopted, which brought together youth service and library staff in a joint training session. The aims of the training were to break down barriers between the services and pair up library staff and youth workers to work together.

Other organisations later came on board, including the Brook Advisory Service. The Children's Services Librarian organised puppet workshops for young mothers to introduce their children to reading and sharing books.

Work with young people continued during *Everybody's Reading*, one highlight being poet Kwame Dawes working with Oldham's African Caribbean project. He encouraged young men to express their views through writing and reading. Library staff are now involved in Oldham's Children's and Youth Alliance Partnership and meet with agencies such as Connexions, Social Services, and Voluntary Action Oldham etc. IT usage is now very popular and young people can access the libraries through the Readers and Writers web site (featured on page 57 of this book).

Project strengths

• All 14 Oldham Libraries have face-on display collections geared to attract young people.

• The number of young people as visitors doubled from November 2001 – August 2002.

• Issue figures for books, music and video trebled, and IT usage increased from 230 to 471 young people.

Everybody's Reading

Contact

Linda Dawson
Outreach and Inclusion Officer

ecs.linda.dawson@oldham.gov.uk
Oldham Library
Union Street
Oldham
OL1 1DN
Tel: 0161 911 4633

Everybody's Reading

High Street Library, Bolton Metropolitan Borough Council
September 2001 – August 2002
Targeting young people aged 16-25 of South Asian Background

Description of Project

As part of the work of the project, 11 events were delivered in libraries and community venues, attracting over 550 young people. Two events were particularly successful:

Books and Bollywood Bonanza
Launch event with silk painting workshop, henna artists, competitions, and performance by a local Asian band. Over 100 people attended.

Makeovers
Staff dressed as fortune tellers and provided reading makeovers (using crystal ball, swinging pendulum) by forecasting what would be read next by twenty people, including the comedian Peter Kay. His attendance ensured good press coverage and added to the credibility of the event with the public.

Feedback from borrower

The library is a bit dull from the outside but Top Stuff inside!

Project Strengths

· Increase in library membership of targeted age range of 25% at High Street library and average of 8% at other service points.

· Development of new partnerships/funding opportunities e.g. European Social Fund, Surestart, Bolton Community College

Weaknesses

· Promoted and created a demand for ICT facilities that could not be satisfied within High Street Library due to building restrictions

Tips for other authorities wishing to repeat idea

· Fortune teller angle seemed to be popular with this age range and proved useful for attracting the press

Contact

Vivian Brown
Team Librarian
Communities and Access

vivian.smith@bolton.gov.uk
Castle Hill Centre
Castleton, Bolton,
BL2 2JW
Tel: 01204 338 123

Books on the Edge

Blackburn Borough Council
April 2004 onwards
Targeting homeless and vulnerable young people

Description of Project

Books on the Edge targets homeless and vulnerable young people, working in partnership with Nightsafe, Blackburn with Darwen Foyer and THOMAS, (Those on the Margins of a Society). A project worker worked for 18.5 hours per week for two years to deliver the project. Satellite collections for use by the target group are being set up in establishments operated by our partners across the Borough. The work builds on foundations laid during the *Everybody's Reading* project.

The project worker concentrates on outreach work, building relationships with the young people we are targeting, before working with them to create collections of material that will be placed in our partners' establishments. The project worker is developing a programme of reader centred activities designed to engage young people and promote literacy. Simultaneously, the Library Management Team are working towards removing barriers which prevent the target group using library services. Staff training will be a major element of the project so that the benefits can be sustained after the funding period has ended.

At every stage young people will be encouraged to be involved in planning and organising activities so that they gain increased confidence and a sense of ownership of the project.

Project Strengths

· Strong partnerships in place to build on work already started.

Weaknesses

· External funding for a period of two years – the project will need to be mainstreamed after that.

Tips for other authorities wishing to repeat idea

· Seek out the experts in the area that you want to work and follow their advice as to what is feasible.

· Make sure the people you are working with are fully involved.

Feedback from outreach worker during Everybody's Reading

I visited a drop-in centre with a selection of books. One of the young women, Tracy, was initially disruptive, pretending to stab other young people who were there. When she saw The Lost Boy *by Dave Pelzer however, she pounced on the book and sat reading it for the rest of the session. She begged to be allowed to keep the book and when it was agreed to keep it for her in the office of the centre she said 'Right, I'll be back at 12.00 tomorrow and at 5 past 12 I'll be reading this book. Don't let anybody else have it.'*

Contact

Geraldine Wilson
Literacy Development Manager

geraldine.wilson@blackburn.gov.uk
Blackburn Central Library
Town Hall Street
Blackburn
BB2 1AG
Tel: 01254 587236

Everybody's Reading and Reading Lifelines

Tameside Metropolitan Borough Council
Hyde Library and Ashton Library 2000 – 2001
Targeting young Asian young people aged 16-25yrs

Description of Project

It was apparent from the outset of the *Everybody's Reading* project that the outreach worker, Rumana Begum had a knack of getting publicity. She was featured in the local papers nearly every week! She already had many contacts with young people living in Hyde and with workers in the area. A poetry competition, graffiti and mehndi workshops were planned as part of the project. *Site Nites* proved to be very popular. Large numbers of young people came to the library to surf the net, borrow books and enjoy activities such as juggling workshops and food and drink were provided by a local restaurant. As part of the project a number of young people interviewed older members of their families and recorded their memories of migration to Hyde from Bangladesh. A booklet, *A Moment in Time* was produced and subsequently an exhibition entitled *Asian Memories* was held at one of the borough's museums. This featured reminiscences, photographs and information about Asian history and culture. The highlight of the project was that Rumana was short listed for the BBC Asian Young Achiever of the Year and the BBC filmed her discussing books with young people at Hyde Library.

Project strengths

· Having a key worker who was well known and liked in the target community.

· Having a budget to finance a range of exciting events and activities.

· Working with a group of people living in one small area made it easier to get information to people and get them involved in library activity.

Weaknesses

· The second phase of the project didn't have quite the same impact, as the co-ordinator was working with more groups, spread over a greater area.

· Many of the links made by the co-ordinator have now been lost and time and resources have not allowed the same input into promoting libraries to this age group since the project.

Tips for other authorities wishing to repeat the idea

· You need commitment at a management level

· Adequate resources

· A key worker with lots of ideas and time to develop links with groups

Contact

Chris Smith
Reader Development Co-ordinator

chris.smith@tameside.gov.uk
Hyde Library
Union St
Hyde
SK14 1NF
Tel: 0161 368 2447

Photo: Ian Lawson. Central Library, Manchester
www.englandsnorthwest.com/

One of the main benefits of a network like Time to Read is that it encourages authorities to share information, but also to explore ways in which they can work practically together. There is a long history of this practice in the UK, the origins of The Reading Agency can be traced back to three library authorities in the South pooling resources. The *Branching Out* project, co-ordinated by *Opening the Book*, has also encouraged people to cross boundaries. An example of this would be the *emrald* (East Midlands Reading and Literature Development) project – a co-operative project taking place between the library authorities in the East Midlands which resulted in a regional reader development strategy.

In the North West of England just two of the ways in which authorities have shared resources are pooled print runs of publicity to provide full colour, high quality material for National Poetry Day. Time To Read has also identified and provided a range of staff training opportunities open to all member authorities.

Crucial benefits of co-operation include economies of scale, not always having to reinvent the wheel and being able to share good, creative ideas across the whole of the region.

Anne Caldwell

Perfect Places Poetry Promotion

Across Time to Read library authorities
Targeting the general public and library users

Description of Project

A number of library authorities asked if the network co-ordinator could produce materials that they could use in their libraries to help promote poetry around National Poetry Day. As the theme for National Poetry Day 2003 was Britain, and as the network represents a specific region, she decided that places in the region should be the focus of the promotion. Material produced was not time-specific, so it could be used to promote poetry beyond National Poetry Day.

A series of high quality, colourful and inspirational posters was created featuring poems inspired by places in NW England, written by poets who live and/or work in NW England. Poets known to librarians were approached and anthologies were searched. Poets were paid for their work through Grants for the Arts from The Arts Council of England.

A series of 10 poems was chosen representing diverse parts of the region.

Time to Read commissioned Manchester Libraries Marketing Unit to design the posters and deliver the finished products. Poets were consulted about the final designs for their posters. 750 sets of posters were produced and 4000 sets of postcards. These were sold at cost price to library authorities across the region.

All 22 authorities purchased some materials. Posters were mainly used in libraries to support displays of poetry books, but were also used generally to brighten buildings, meeting rooms and at external events. Some authorities chose to send their posters to other council buildings, schools etc. Postcards generally were given out on National Poetry Day and at related events.

Using the posters ensured that poetry was promoted in many libraries across the region, and extra poetry books were bought for displays.

Project strengths

· Quality and range of poems and designs

· Producing in large quantity brings economy in costs

· Encouraged libraries to promote poetry when they might not have done so otherwise

· Long lead-in time meant an ambitious project was achievable

Weaknesses

· Choice of poems was a bit haphazard, based on who and what we knew

· 10 was probably too ambitious in one year

· Forgot to budget for delivery – costs and time

· Not marketed beyond library services - this can be rectified in year two

Feedback from authorities

Stockport: *We put them in all the usual places plus the Town Hall. No-one has taken them down so they are still there! When the promotion was finished I received many enquiries about them, could town hall staff have them and where could people buy them from. The library staff loved them. They had a set of ten per library and I think most of the staff took those.*

Warrington: *Just to let you know about the more unusual kind of places Warrington displayed the posters: lots of pubs, taxi ranks, laundrettes and we even gave some to the Ranger service to display on trees in open spaces throughout the area.*

Tips for other authorities wishing to repeat idea

· Talk to arts officers / writers groups about how to select poems
· Use a designer you have a lot of confidence in
· Retain final control over choice of designs and images

Contact

Jane Mathieson
Time to Read Co-ordinator

nwreader@libraries.manchester.gov.uk
c/o Manchester Central Library
St Peter's Square
Manchester
M2 5PD
Tel: 0161 236 4451

time to read
North West Libraries Reader Development Partnership

COUNCIL
ENGLAND
OTTERY FUNDED

National Poetry Day Co-ordinated Events

National Poetry Day, 9th October 2003
Six co-ordinated events in Rochdale, Warrington, Manchester, Stockport, Tameside, Bolton
Targeting general public and school age children.

Description of Project

Manchester Poetry Festival (MPF) has worked in partnership with Manchester Libraries for nine years to put on an accessible, imaginative, city centre event on National Poetry Day and for several years has received sponsorship funding from Manchester Airport. In 2003 MPF had also received regional arts lottery funding to support events outside the city centre.

Working with the Time to Read co-ordinator, MPF wanted to support a wider range of activity and had gained additional commitment from Manchester Airport.
Time to Read authorities were asked if they wished to participate in a co-ordinated activity and six authorities were chosen – those directly affected by the Airport - Tameside, Stockport, Warrington and Manchester, plus Bolton and Rochdale to the north of the city.

A small team of representatives from each authority met with the MPF co-ordinator, who outlined the sort of event being looked for and discussed a range of possible activities.

Funding from MPF paid for staging and PA equipment, a host poet for the whole day and two visiting celebrity poets who each visited three stages.

Authorities were asked to put on a daytime event in a shopping centre or outside a library, publicise and invite potential audience and design a day of performance poetry using local writers groups and schools.

Members of the public were encouraged to read poems and/or listen to poems being read. At Warrington's event 60 people read their own work during the day. Six stages happened for poetry readings and performances approx 10-3.30pm in each venue.

In addition a poetry performance was given by Ian McMillan in the Library Theatre, Manchester, for an invited school audience. 6,000 goody bags were provided by Manchester Airport.

MANCHESTER
POETRY
FESTIVAL

Feedback from audiences

I never knew there were so many poets in our town. We should use this centre for more events like this.
Sultan Ali, Mayor of Rochdale

National Poetry Day 2003 in Warrington showed us how much talent and interest in poetry there is in the town. People spent hours sitting in the shopping centre, listening and participating in the event, which was led by a brilliant MC. Following this we have set up a lively poetry reading group at Warrington Library.
Feedback from staff

Project strengths

· Co-ordination of poets, hosts and equipment meant some authorities were encouraged to try something for the first time.
· Getting commitment from schools to attend is difficult, but it makes all the difference and brings the generations together.
· Using Manchester Poetry Festival expertise meant hosts and guest poets were experienced.

Weaknesses

· Using outdoor venues is stressful and can lead to disaster if wet.
· Some shopping centre managers were not sufficiently supportive - led to one stage being tucked away in a corner.

Tips for other authorities wishing to repeat idea

· Don't make your day too long. Short and snappy is better than long and full of gaps.
· Talk to people who have done it before.
· Involve writers' groups and encourage them to attend.
· Encourage schools to write or practise something to bring with them.

Contact

Jane Mathieson
Time to Read Co-ordinator

nwreader@libraries.manchester.gov.uk
c/o Manchester Central Library
St Peter's Square
Manchester,
M2 5PD
Tel: 0161 236 4451

Fly the Flag for Poetry

Rochdale Metropolitan Borough
A more detailed example of regionally supported events for National Poetry Day 2003.
The Wheatsheaf Shopping Centre, Rochdale
Targeting shoppers and primary school children.

Description of Project

Fly the Flag for Poetry was hosted by poet Suki Mitchell. The Mayor of Rochdale, Sultan Ali also came along to give his support and to read *Daffodils* – voted favourite poem by the Wheatsheaf Library's customers. Local poets who performed on the day were Sue Holt, Jan Lingard and Norma Tweedle.

Roving poet for the day was Owen Sheers, who came to the event at lunchtime.

Library staff read poems nominated by library users, and so did the school children who attended. In the afternoon, people were invited up on stage to read their favourite work, and more local poets read. 142 shoppers stopped to listen. 285 children from six schools attended. We received 64 competition entries (flags and poems) from children.

Feedback from audience

Both my friend Linda and myself enjoyed taking part in the Poetry Day at the Wheatsheaf Centre **participant** who sent a letter to the area librarian in poem form as a way of saying thank you!

Project Strengths

· Participation of the mayor raised the event's status with the Borough Council
· Partnerships with local schools
· The venue, and co-operation from the Centre management

Weaknesses

· Not enough seating
· Lack of interest from local press

Tips for other authorities wishing to repeat idea

· Don't have tannoy announcements advertising the event as poets are reciting!

Contact

Janice Tod
Area Librarian Rochdale and Per

janice.tod@rochdale.gov.uk
The Wheatsheaf Library
Baillie St
Rochdale
OL16 1JZ
Tel: 01706 864976

high time in Rochdale

black elephants
    jazz dancing
gold and red
grin.
I imagine they wave
as they pass the window
of my third floor flat.
just in case they are
I wave back.

Shamshad Khan

Example of Perfect Places Poetry Postcard see page 15

Photo: Ian Lawson. The Golden Gates, Warrington
www.englandsnorthwest.com/

Chapter Three   Bringing Readers Together

There has been an explosion of interest in reading groups in the UK in recent years, and much of this interest has been generated by library authorities. Within this region, libraries have set up many groups themselves. They have also publicised and supported externally run groups and set up services such as loan collections to support their work. The consequence has been that readers don't have to feel isolated, and can easily find groups of like-minded individuals to join. One library member of staff reported back to me: "Our reading group has now been going for five years. They will tackle anything chucked in their direction and are very adventurous."

Both publishers and the national media realise the importance of this new audience for books, with the popularity of TV book slots on *Richard and Judy*, and publishers such as Penguin supporting the development reading groups via the web. The challenge for authorities now is to make the best use of these reading advocates, and come up with creative ways of using their skills within the service. Libraries also face the challenge of involving a wider cross-section of the community in their reading group provision. Examples of different approaches are included in this chapter.

Anne Caldwell

Tips for other authorities wishing to repeat idea

· Be prepared to spend a long time building trust and confidence.

· Don't give up just because only one or two people come along at first.

· Word of mouth is a powerful draw.

· Just two enthusiasts can bring in others over a period of time.

Contact

Geraldine Wilson
Literacy Development Manager

geraldine.wilson@blackburn.gov.uk
Blackburn Central Library
Town Hall St
Blackburn
BB2 1AG
Tel: 01254 587236

Asian Women's Reading Group

Blackburn Borough Council
Bangor Street Health Centre and Seven Trees Family Centre, Blackburn
June 2001 – ongoing, targeting Asian women

Description of Project

Several groups are run by the library service in Blackburn, some in partnership with other agencies. This group is run with the Lifelong Learning Service and the Health Service. Originally held in a local health centre, health visitors invited a number of women to join as they see the group as promoting mental and social well-being. The women read books in English and many have not read for pleasure since leaving school. As their reading has developed, it has also enabled women to talk openly on other issues and use each other for support.

Initially some women were hesitant about reading again. It is a sign of growing confidence and self-esteem that two women put in a successful application for a Reading Families Millennium Award. They will now promote reading within the Asian community informally through play groups and in other women's homes. The Library and Information Service will support them with guidance on books, other partners will provide mentoring. The group as a whole has now outgrown the health centre and has moved to a Social Services family centre where there is more space for children to play. All have joined the library for themselves and for their children, read widely and recommend books to each other on a regular basis.

Feedback from members

When Alison (the health visitor) asked me to come along it was like I'd made a wish and it had come true.

Project Strengths

· The venue – in the community and a safe place to visit.

· Partnerships – health visitors did outreach work.

Weaknesses

· Very slow process to build up numbers because of social issues.

· Lack of funding for crèche facilities.

· Gets very hectic in the group because toys, children and mothers are in the same room.

Young People's Reading Group - Pilot Project

Stockport Local Authority
Edgeley Library, Stockport September 2003 – ongoing
Targeting young people aged 13-16yrs

Description of Project

It was recognised that a reading group aimed at this age group would need to be significantly different to our adult oriented groups, not only in terms of what was read but also how we marketed the group and how the meetings would be organised. What we didn't want to do was assume what young people wanted or what would appeal to them. Were we to miss the mark the result could be perceived by the intended audience as passé or patronising and the whole initiative be doomed from the start. It was therefore decided from the outset to get members of the target audience involved in the planning of the group.

We were very fortunate to find two enthusiastic young people, Gabrielle (aged 14) and Matt (aged 15) both of whom were keen to get involved. We held four planning meetings with Gaby and Matt. Their contributions were invaluable and formed the basis of all that followed. Examples of their direct contribution include:

· Avoid the term 'reading group' in publicity – this sounds too formal and school-like.

· Short, snappy 'brand' name for the group – the name 'Edge' (as short for Edgeley) was chosen.

· Times of meetings: It was decided that 5pm on a week day would be good, giving members time to get home from school/college and to the library. We also decided to meet when the library was closed. This would mean we had the 'run of the library' without worrying about making noise and also opened up the possibility of playing CDs or watching videos etc.

Since the launch in September 2003, the group has proved very successful with an active group of regular attendees. Feedback from the group has been very positive and their continued attendance suggests we must be doing something right!

Feedback from participant

I think the idea of a teenage reading group is great. It provides a place for people to go to talk about books
Sindy (14)

edge; a readers' gathering

Project strengths

· Successfully targets a traditionally hard to reach section of the community

· Provides an opportunity for young people to talk about books away from the more formal setting of school

· Provides us with a group for consultation purposes

· The group has been taken to Borders bookshop with a budget of £700 to choose books for their area in Edgeley Library. These were displayed as a promotion as chosen by *Edge* and were all issued within three days. We bought a duplicate copy of the promotion to rotate throughout Stockport Libraries to promote the group, give kudos to the group and promote the message that young people can have a direct influence in the books that are stocked.

Weaknesses

· So far the group consists mainly of young people who already used the library. We need to try and attract some non-users.

· Very aware of finite length of appeal to existing members. Need to be constantly promoting to keep up numbers as existing members 'grow out of it'.

Tips for other authorities wishing to repeat idea

· Get young people involved in the planning process.

· Don't be afraid of informality in the meetings and don't be surprised if the majority of the meeting time is spent talking about things other than the books – at least they are reading the books.

· Get enthusiastic staff on board – people who don't mind making fools of themselves or being made to feel very, very old!

Contact

Paul Howarth
Librarian (Cultural Impact)

paul.howarth@stockport.gov.uk
Phoenix House
Birdhall Lane
Cheadle Heath, Stockport
SK3 0RA
Tel: 0161 474 5751

Reading Group Loan Collection
Cumbria Libraries 2002 – ongoing
Targeting reading groups in Cumbria

Description of Project

Many reading groups in Cumbria were coming in to request multiple copies of the same novel. It was a complex process for the request service to co-ordinate sufficient copies from the system. Several would be out on loan at a given time. A reading group member who had moved into Cumbria handed in a comment form which described a loan collection service in Hertfordshire and in response to this obvious need, it was decided to set up a centralised county collection. This would consist of sets of multiple copies of novels for reading groups to borrow. An initial 40 contemporary and classic titles were identified and a budget of £2,000 was allocated to the project.

Ten copies of each title were bought in paperback, and the collection includes adult and children's titles. It is located in Carlisle library alongside well-established music and drama loans services.

The service was promoted via the county library website, hard copy lists in libraries and a publicity mail shot to reading groups. A promotional leaflet with a teabag stuck inside was sent to groups to emphasise the social aspects of reading!

Sets can be requested at any service point, and are free. They are delivered to the nearest library for a reading group member to collect and can be kept for up to six months. In December 2003, the county appointed a Reader Development Officer, who now has overall responsibility for the collections.

Feedback from reading group member

This service enables our reading group to have access to a range of familiar books, but also to more diverse and even challenging titles.

Project strengths

- Filled gap in service provision, responded to need
- Very popular and effective
- Less strain on request service
- Range of choice for reading groups to borrow
- Information on website helps groups make informed choices

Weaknesses

- We are a victim of our own success – waiting lists for some sets
- Needs regular financial input, needs to be budgeted for
- Takes up staff time

Tips for other authorities wanting to repeat idea

· Thoroughly plan how to administer the service before setting it up.

· 10 copies per set is not enough – we have now upped this to 12.

· Free requests encourage use of the service and are more inclusive.

· Think about needs of visually impaired readers – we have used the system to obtain copies in talking book format for one particular reading group.

· Consult widely on suggestions for titles.

· Include children's titles and cross-over books that appeal to adults and young people.

· On the website, we have included images of book titles and plot summaries.

Contact

Helen Towers
Reader Development Officer

helen.towers@cumbriacc.gov.uk
Arroyo Block
The Castle
Carlisle
Cumbria CA3 8UR
Tel: 01228 607287

Description of project

Since 1998 the number of reading groups in St Helens has increased from one to seven.

Most groups have evolved from general publicity at libraries and are currently run by library staff. Books are supplied by the library service and each evening revolves around discussion on a particular book, and refreshments.

We also ran a group for staff for approximately one year. The small group met regularly to discuss books they each suggested. All the staff enjoyed the meetings, discussions continued outside the group and everyone said they read books they wouldn't normally read.

The group only ceased to meet following a restructure when many members changed their base library. A new group may start in the future.

Project strengths

· Members have opportunity to meet liked-minded people.

· Can discuss books they've enjoyed (or hated!).

· The groups stimulate people to try different authors and persevere with more demanding books.

· Staff widened their reading knowledge.

Weaknesses

· Difficult to sometimes keep conversation focused on books.

· Reaching small audience as each group can only accommodate up to 10 people.

· Difficult to get copies of books quickly.

· Sometimes left with copies that don't issue very well.

· Staff groups fold when people change their workplace.

Contact

Jane E Rimmer
Team Librarian, Reading & Learning

janeerimmer@sthelens.gov.uk
Rainhill Library
View Road
Rainhill
L35 0LE
Tel: 01744 677822

Description of Project

This is a new group initiated through public interest which meets to share the pleasure and enjoyment of reading poetry. The group originally planned to meet monthly but has proved so popular that it now meets every fortnight. Members are encouraged to bring along poems to read aloud, and share with others. These can be poems people have written themselves, or published ones. Members often bring material written by their children or grandchildren. The leader always has plenty of material to fill in the gaps. There is no obligation to attend every meeting, tea and biscuits are provided and there is no charge.

Feedback from group member

Everyone enjoys it so much, it's really fun!

Project Strengths

· Led by member of the public

· Enthusiastic leader

· Helping to forge community spirit and focusing library as the centre of the community

Tips for other authorities wishing to repeat idea

· Stress that people don't have to write poetry, although for those that do their poems are very welcome.

· All welcome – people don't have to read out loud, they can just listen.

· Stress the fun element – the poetry we share is light-hearted rather than literary, although this may develop if the group wishes over time.

· Choose a theme each week – e.g. animals, flowers, food, childhood.

· People bring poems they've seen in books, magazines or written themselves.

Contact

Janice Tod
Area Librarian Rochdale and Pennines

janice.tod@rochdale.gov.uk
The Wheatsheaf Library
Baillie St
Rochdale
OL16 1JZ
Tel: 01706 864976

Photo: Ian Lawson. Salford Quays Skyline
www.englandsnorthwest.com/

The status and impact of reader development work has been greatly enhanced in recent years by a more strategic approach from national agencies and library authorities. On a national level, this has led to an increase in funding, and profile for the work, and the involvement of media, such as the BBC. Publishers and those organisations who administer major prizes are also beginning to see the benefits of getting libraries on board, such as the Man Booker Prize and Orange Prize for fiction.

For some authorities in the North West, there has almost been an embarrassment of riches in this field, with services stretched to keep up with the wealth of new opportunities. As with all new partnerships there have been some initial teething troubles around adapting to new challenges. Having said that, reading has never been so sexy, nor had so much media coverage and our services are very well placed to exploit this interest.

Anne Caldwell

Description of Project

Over 13,000 people were caught reading on World Book Day in Salford in more than 60 different organisations.

To engage different groups with reading, the Libraries and Information Service set up an offer that organisations could buy into. On offer were free resources (T-shirts, balloons, certificates and stickers), plus the opportunity to enter a prize draw to win £100 of books. The promotion enabled different organisations to focus on reading for one day.

Joint working between the Reader Development Officer, the Schools Library Service and the Children's team (including Bookstart Officers) led to 60 different organisations getting involved from the many different sectors. All those involved organised their own event with support from library staff. An added incentive was the ability to maximise publicity for their organisation because of other high profile events in libraries. Events ranged from personal visits by renowned authors such as Melvin Burgess and Adèle Geras to sponsored reads, bouncing stories, book chats and story times.

Target groups included

· High Schools, and primary schools

· FE Colleges

· Probation Services (Youth Offending Team)

· Community Centres

· Voluntary agencies

· Other council teams (Community Safety Unit)

· Work-based learning providers

Feedback on the project

I was in several offices on World Book Day - in all sorts of places across the city - and they all seemed to have had the badges or balloons for World Book Day. **Head of Culture and Heritage**

The certificates and stickers were a great success. It was good to see our children taking them home proudly, after they had all been involved in a book related activity of some sort during the day and all been "caught reading" in Salford! **School Librarian**

Project strengths

• Optional participation by community groups

• Providing a ready-made package to supplement what many would be doing anyway (especially schools) but which particularly interested the press because it was so extensive.

• Linking in with national project. This gave the local festival more clout and in addition the World Book Day Online Festival website from 2003 was shown as an example of what could be done on World Book Day. The online festival helped us to get a feature on the council's home page and also helped us make links between libraries and youth services which we feel will be productive for future projects.

Tips for other authorities wishing to repeat idea

• Ensure library staff have an opportunity to input into the project so that they own it.

• Make sure designs are big and bold.

Contact

Janet Swan
Reader Development Officer

janet.swan@salford.gov.uk
Eccles Library
Church Street
Eccles
M30 0EP
Tel. 0161 707 9612

Description of Project

For the first time in Wirral two reading groups from libraries at West Kirby and Upton shadowed the Orange Prize nominations for 2004. Copies of the long listed books were provided and reading groups were encouraged by enthusiastic library staff to read as many titles as possible. Group members selected titles they wanted to discuss at their meetings and books could be read and exchanged at any time.

Heated discussion and impassioned recommendation was often the order of the day, some members read more than others, some got stuck and were encouraged to finish by other readers, others lead the way by their enthusiastic advocacy of one title or another. The books were kept for the reading groups allowing them to have a good chance to read as many of the long and short listed titles as they could. In addition other titles were made available throughout 24 libraries so that other reading groups could also take part.

A grand Orange party was planned for the night of the announcement; we invited readers from all of our adult reading groups to a library with an orange glow!
A woman dressed in black with a bikini over her t-shirt made of orange skins and orange twine was a real show stopper! The atmosphere was very festive and the discussion and argument was animated. The National winner was announced on the dot at 8pm to great applause, Wirral's own choice for this year's winner was as follows:

Rose Tremain – *The Colour* 1st Place   **Andrea Leavy** – *Small Island* – 2nd Place

We thoroughly enjoyed our first foray into the joys of shadowing and fully intend to do it again next year.

Feedback from participants

A reader recovering from cancer read all of the titles, she said it gave her a focus and was something she could do for herself. She had enjoyed every minute.

Staff loved the interaction, and the fact that they were part of a national network for reading actively judging with the real judges

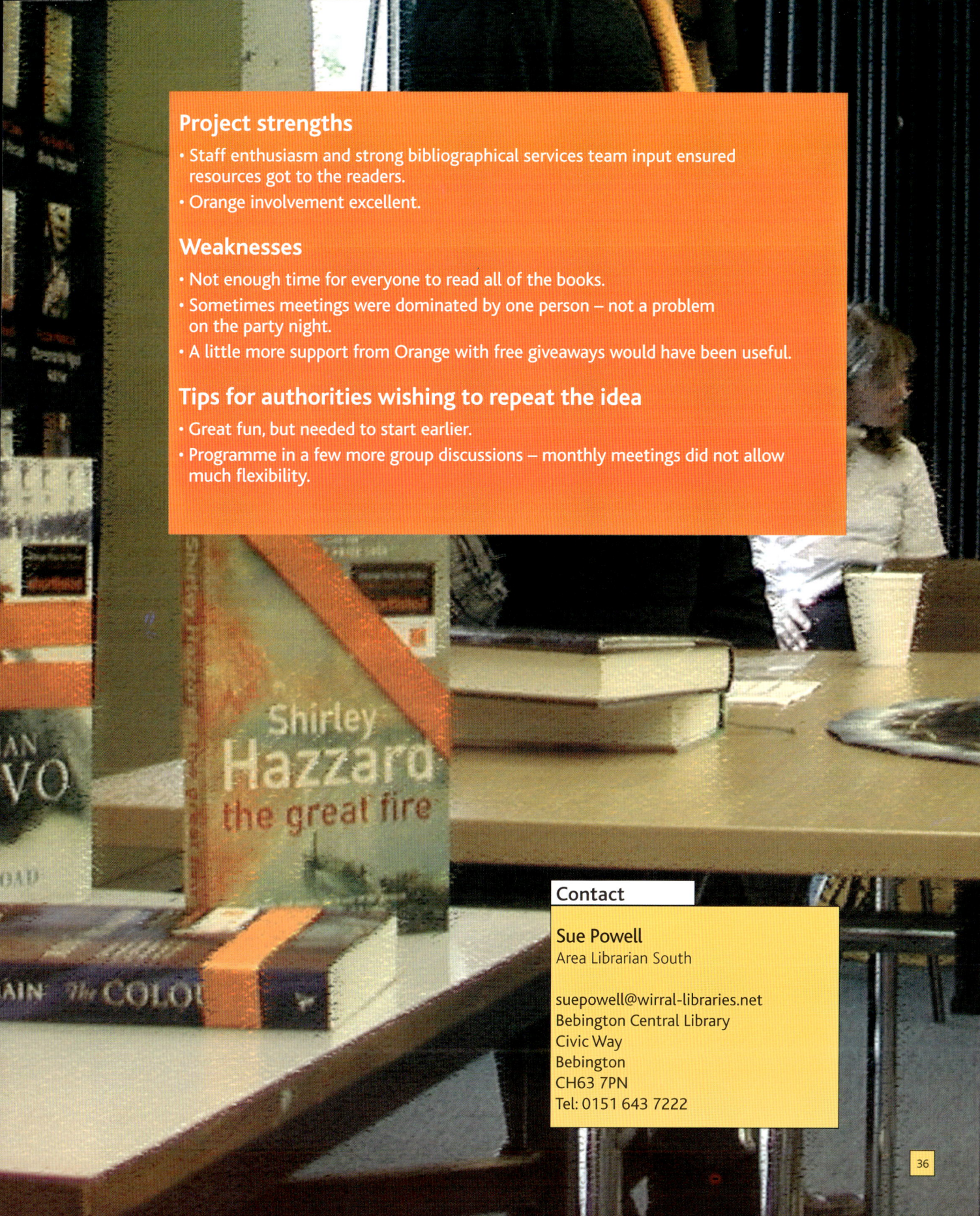

Project strengths

• Staff enthusiasm and strong bibliographical services team input ensured resources got to the readers.

• Orange involvement excellent.

Weaknesses

• Not enough time for everyone to read all of the books.

• Sometimes meetings were dominated by one person – not a problem on the party night.

• A little more support from Orange with free giveaways would have been useful.

Tips for authorities wishing to repeat the idea

• Great fun, but needed to start earlier.

• Programme in a few more group discussions – monthly meetings did not allow much flexibility.

Contact

Sue Powell
Area Librarian South

suepowell@wirral-libraries.net
Bebington Central Library
Civic Way
Bebington
CH63 7PN
Tel: 0151 643 7222

The Big Read

St Helens Borough Council
Throughout St Helen's April 2003, targeting children, staff and adults

Description of Project

The BBC's *Big Read* campaign inspired us to organise a range of events to promote reading in 2003. During April, all libraries had *Big Read* displays and staff took part in a competition to match their Top 21 with the actual Top 21. In the autumn campaign, libraries put up displays of the Top 21 and the public were invited to vote for the best loved book. Children were asked to draw their own book worm. In the focus week, we held a *Big Read* do at Central Library and members of the public came and took part in a quiz, enjoyed readings and drank wine. In the same week a new staff reading group was set up.

Feedback from library reading group member

...really enjoyed that evening - when are we doing it again?

Project strengths

• A great way to promote books and reading
• Quality of publicity materials very high
• Good general media coverage

Weaknesses

• Activities perhaps seen as one-offs relating only to *The Big Read*
• The nature of the top 21 seemed limited

Tips for authorities wishing to repeat idea

• Nibbles sufficient, plus wine and soft drinks
• The Top 21 quiz seemed to work well and gave people a chance to walk around and chat to each other (quiz pictures were stuck on the walls and shelves around the library).
• People enjoyed answering general questions about their reading.

Contact

Jane E Rimmer
Team Librarian, Reading & Learning

janeerimmer@sthelens.gov.uk
Rainhill Library
View Road
Rainhill
L35 0LE
Tel: 01744 677822

The Big Read Summer Sunday Readings
Liverpool City Council
Sefton Park Palm House, Liverpool 2 – 3 pm from 13th July – 14th September 2003
targeting readers of all ages and backgrounds

Description of Project

Liverpool Libraries and Information Services teamed up with *The Reader* magazine to present a series of Sunday afternoon readings in Sefton Park Palm House featuring the nation's 100 favourite books nominated during the BBC's *Big Read* project.

Each week there were readings from four of the top 100 books. Readers were members of the public aged between nine and ninety who wanted to read an extract from their favourite *Big Read* nomination. The readings amongst the palms proved popular despite the tropical temperatures on some hot Sundays. A regular audience developed and it is estimated that approximately 1500 people attended the readings.

There was a library stall and the top 100 *Big Read* books were loaned to readers and dozens of new members were enrolled. Waterstones and *The Reader* also had stalls and there were colouring and drawing activities for children and lots of publishers' giveaways.

The success of the project encouraged us to arrange *Tasty Reads* from the top 21 books in the Central Library in conjunction with Radio Merseyside. Presenters and volunteers gave bite-sized readings from their favourite books during lunchtime readings. The sessions were recorded and broadcast as a programme on Radio Merseyside over the Christmas holiday.

The project showed that people enjoy listening to readings. It enabled us to reach out to new audiences and to promote the library service in a novel setting. The Radio Merseyside tie-in helped us win valuable publicity for the service throughout the city.

Feedback from audience
The readings are a real indulgence for me, it's a real luxury just sitting here and being read to.

Project strengths
· It was fairly cheap to arrange – just the cost of publicity and a part-time organiser who arranged the reading volunteers.
· The readings in the novel setting of the Palm House enabled us to reach a new audience and enrol new members.
· The Radio Merseyside connection delivered some quality and entertaining events in the Central Library and won some excellent free publicity.
· The initiative won praise from councillors and high ranking council officials who happened to visit the Palm House.

Weaknesses
· Some of the readers were of a very high calibre, but others failed to grab the audience's attention.
· There were a few technical problems with the PA system on a couple of Sundays.
· Some visitors may not have noticed the library connection despite our stall and the library publicity display.

Tips for other authorities wishing to repeat idea
· You need an organiser with a good network of contacts to attract reading volunteers, someone who knows how to grab publicity.
· You need an attractive, comfortable and informal venue where people will linger.

Contact

Ron Travis
Manager, Community Libraries

ron.travis@liverpool.gov.uk
Liverpool Central Library
William Brown St
Liverpool
L3 8EW
Tel: 0151 233 5847

Description of Project

Using *The Big Read* as a hook, and appointing Joy Winkler as a 'Big Reader in Residence', reader development work took place in seven priority libraries in the county. Joy worked with the libraries over a four month period to plan and organise promotions and events that tied in with the campaign. The events mostly took place in the Libraries' focus week in early December. They ranged from coffee mornings, evenings that included informal discussions around the Top 21, balloon debates and more traditional reading group discussions. Quizzes, local ballots, book sales and displays were also created to help with publicity. For example, Bollington Library drew inspiration from its local landmark, a triangulation point called The White Nancy. Readers were invited to plot their Big Reads with footprints up towards the summit! In addition to good attendance and excellent audience feedback, two new library-based reading groups were set up at Handforth.

Feedback from staff member

It got everybody talking about books and reading. Staff and public seem much keener to talk about books they read and recommend books to each other. Got staff working together on projects and encouraged them to put forward ideas to promote stock and services.

Project strengths

· Successful activities have built confidence to do something similar again

· Made staff think about how to get involved in future national promotions

· Encourage staff to talk to each other and borrowers about books

· Increased team working

Weaknesses

· Promotion went on too long

· Difficult in some cases to maintain momentum

Tips for other authorities wishing to repeat the idea

· Useful to appoint an external reader in residence

· Enabled focused and strategic reader development to take place in the libraries given priority status

· A fresh approach was created

Contact

Elizabeth Newall
Literature & Reading Development Officer

elizabeth.newall@cheshire.gov.
Goldsmith House
Hamilton Place
Chester, CH1 1SE
Tel: 01244 602898

Bolton's Big Read

Bolton Metropolitan Borough, Summer & Autumn 2003
Targeting readers and non-members, children and adults

Description of Project

Bolton Libraries decided to promote a local vote for *Bolton's Big Read* in addition to displaying and promoting the BBC Top 21 titles.

Big Read Tea Parties were held in libraries with free tea and cake, to encourage people to vote and discuss their voting choices. Voting was also possible during normal opening hours.

Adult and junior competitions were held and extra copies of the BBC Top 21 were purchased.

Feedback from reader

I never thought I would want to pick up War and Peace, but I'm really glad I did.

Project strengths

· The Bolton vote gave staff an opportunity to include a wider range of stock in the displays, reflecting the multi-cultural society we serve and promoting some lesser-known local authors or NW based titles.

· The national publicity, as well as local displays, had an obvious effect on the issues: comparative statistics for the autumn 2002 showed a four or five-fold increase for some titles.

Tips for other authorities wishing to repeat idea

· Engage press interest from an early stage to promote the project, as local papers are always interested in stories with a local angle

Contact

Vivian Brown
Communities & Access Librarian

vivian.brown@bolton.gov.uk
Castle Hill Centre
Bolton, BL2 2JW
Tel: 01204 332417

Voting and Yet More Voting

The Big Read in Tameside Metropolitan Borough
Targeting all readers across the Borough 2003

Description of Project

Tameside found a range of creative ways to take part in *The Big Read* in 2003. Displays, readers' group discussions, a fun quiz and a 'Big Book Chat' were routes to support the public to re-read old favourites and try new authors. Staff worked enthusiastically to encourage people to vote for their favourite book and this paid dividends: Tameside Central Library became the number one public library voting spot in the country! A large worm crawled towards Tameside in recognition of this achievement (courtesy of the BBC) and now resides in the library, pictured opposite with library worker Lynda Reavey.

Not to be outdone, staff at Audenshaw Library spotted the great prizes offered in the WH Smith People's Choice Book Awards. They enthused their customers to cast their votes, and this resulted in another number one spot and a trip to The Dorchester for the Awards Ceremony for two staff members.

Feedback from library customer

It's got me reading old favourites that I first read years ago and now I'm going to join a reading group!

Project strengths

- Few resources needed and not too staff intensive
- Good for publicity – we got a lot of coverage from local papers, CILIP and Council publications
- Great for staff morale
- Linked ICT and reader development

Weaknesses

- Needed to be able to enthuse staff to encourage customers to vote
- Many members of the public didn't have time or didn't want to vote

Tips for other authorities wishing to repeat idea

- Put details of the promotion on the Council intranet and encourage people to cast their vote
- Ask everyone who comes into the library whether they would like to vote
- Help people to vote
- Have the voting site as home page on computers in libraries
- Offer incentives – e.g. sweets given to people who vote!
- Remind people at events such as story times, readers' groups etc
- Ensure that the library staff vote

Contact

Chris Smith
Reader Development Co-ordinator

chris.smith@tameside.gov.uk
Hyde Library
Union Street
Hyde SK14 1NF
Tel: 0161 368 2447

Photo: Manchester Library & Information Service, Alderley Edge, Cheshire

Along with other arts providers, libraries share the challenge of maintaining and attracting audiences for their services – this can simply include getting people through the door, but also encouraging them to take part in the wealth of artistic activities that libraries put on – readings, readers' groups, festivals, live literature events, reader-focused websites and lively programmes of reader-centred work for children.

When I have spoken to library staff up and down the country, one of their biggest concerns has been the view that the traditional library audience is aging, and libraries need to encourage younger people, particularly young adults, to see the service as relevant to their lives. Libraries are often juggling the need to keep their existing readers while also attracting a younger readership. The following chapter outlines positive ways in which authorities are meeting this challenge.

Anne Caldwell

World Book Day Shenanigans

Cheshire County Council, Bollington and Malpas Libraries – 3rd and 4th March 2004.
Targeting young people and families

Description of Project

To help promote and celebrate World Book Day 2004, Cheshire's Rural Touring Network invited the dance company, Ascendance, to undertake a two day residency in Cheshire libraries. Forty young people took part from local schools. Rural Touring Network audiences and the families of the participants watched the shows. The company worked with two separate groups of twenty young people, leading workshops in the library spaces during opening hours, and drawing inspiration from the library setting. In order to draw particular attention to the World Book Day Online Reading Festival, the dance company was asked to draw out themes, story lines and characters from a book by one of the featured authors in the festival. The company worked from Jamila Gavin's novel *The Track of the Wind*. The young people and the dance company concluded both days by performing their original pieces to public audiences.

Feedback from participants

It was a bit weird dancing in a library, but it was fun and the public saw our routine!
Young person from the project

It was truly inspiring to see such an incredibly imaginative interpretation of a book and to see the library space used so creatively, and be so animated! Staff member

Project strengths

· Helped promote World Book Day
· Introduced participants and audience to a different way of interpreting a reading experience and using library spaces.
· Strong partnership
· Very professional dance company
· Commitment from library staff, especially given that workshops took place in opening hours

Weaknesses

· Dance company quite late in deciding which book to use
· Not much time to source extra copies to promote/issue on the day to participants

Tips for other authorities wishing to repeat idea

· Find appropriate partners if you haven't got the funds to finance the entire project cost
· Ask the dance company to inform you of their book choice
  well in advance.

Contact

Elizabeth Newall
Literature & Reading
Development Officer

elizabeth.newall@cheshire.gov.uk
Goldsmith House
Hamilton Place
Chester, CH1 1SE
Tel: 01244 602898

Photo: Courtesy of Cheshire County Council Arts Service

Bury Bonus Cards

Bury Metropolitan Borough Council
Throughout authority, October 2003 - ongoing
Targeting all library users and junior members

Description of Project

We wanted to give some incentive and recognition to our regular borrowers as well as a little encouragement to keep new members coming back. Each time they borrow, they receive a stamp: six stamps earn one point, one point earns a free reservation, two points, a free audio-visual loan. At first we just thought of giving free audio-visual loans but we decided to include reservations because our core business is books. We also hoped that this would encourage people to ask for titles they didn't find on the shelves.

The cards were designed internally and printed in-house on brightly coloured card. They are displayed prominently at issue counters, together with the poster. They are also given to all new borrowers. A5 was chosen as being a suitable size to keep inside a book.

Draws for book tokens are held approximately every three months.

The scheme was a national first and thanks to our enthusiastic new press officer the launch featured a local councillor stamping a giant version of the card. This attracted coverage in the professional press as well as local papers and brought enquiries from other authorities who were thinking of copying it.

Feedback from borrowers

What a good idea, thank you!

Project strengths
· Cheap and easy to administer
· Popular with staff and borrowers
· Excellent public relations

Weaknesses
· Staff don't always remember to ask people if they have a card, particularly at busy times; this could be solved by linking the scheme to the circulation system but cost and technical considerations mean that there are no plans for this.

Tips for other authorities wishing to repeat idea
· Keep it simple

Contact

Maxine Goda
Assistant Librarian, Reader Development

maxineG@bury.gov.uk
Bury Metro Libraries
Radcliffe Library
Stand Lane
M26 1NW
Tel: 0161 253 7163

Poetry4Life

Lancashire County Council
Preston, Lancashire National Poetry Day 2003 - Collections still ongoing
Particularly targeting young black people for participation, and adult readers for poetry collections

Description of Project

Over a period of six months, twenty young people from the city of Preston and the surrounding area made poetry films, inspired by poems they had read and written themselves. The films were screened at the Warner/Vue Cinema in Preston with full 'Oscars' treatment on National Poetry Day 2003, to an audience of over 50 people that included all the local press and three mayors!

The films included parachute adventures, a science fiction fantasy, nightmare dreams and shadow puppets made by young people from the Foxton Titans Youth Group, Avenham, the Nguzo Saba Centre in Preston and Clayton Brook Homework Club. At the same time brand new collections of contemporary poetry were introduced at three Lancashire Libraries.

Poetry4Life was coordinated by the arts company Sources, which is run by poet Anne Caldwell and artist Jack Lockhart. Anne operated as Poet-in-residence and Jack was employed for half a day a week as Filmmaker-in-Residence. The project was supported by Vue Cinema and the Arts Council of England.

Eye-catching publicity was produced including good quality posters and leaflets. The new collections of poetry which were bought are attractive and cover a wide range of tastes. They were selected after a visit to Waterstones in Manchester, The Poetry Library in London and research into small presses. Sources also shared their expertise with the stock promotion library staff. All the stock purchased is continuing to issue well and customer feedback is very positive.

Feedback on the project

We really enjoyed seeing our ideas come to life! **Member of the Foxton Titans youth group**

It was great to go to Waterstones and look at the book covers – it enthused me to promote the stock we chose. **Library staff member**

My group could not believe it when they saw their work on in a cinema – it was something they could never have imagined. **Youth Worker**

Contact

Alison Thies
Service Development Officer

Alison.Thies@lcl.lancscc.gov.uk
Room D21, Lancashire County Council
County Hall
Preston, PR1 8XJ
Tel: 01772 534051

Project strengths

· The quality of the stock, both in content and attractiveness – use a bookseller with a large collection so you know what the stock looks like.

· Involving the young people in a project which gave them a chance to show off their talents, whilst developing their reading, new media, IT and creative writing skills.

· Three new collections of over 300 contemporary poetry books for libraries

Weaknesses

· Problems of supply when dealing with small presses, not well organised to supply material and are slow to respond to messages – plan well in advance!

· Tying together the two strands of the promotion which didn't seem to come together until the launch when the films were shown in the cinema.

Tips for other authorities wishing to repeat idea

· Use experts even if you have to pay
· Plan well in advance – the stock can take time to pull together.

come and sample a new collection
of *life*-enhancing poetry at a library near you

Wargames Events for Teenagers

Sefton Metropolitan Borough Council
First event autumn 2003 at Formby Library, ongoing
Targeting young people (especially boys) aged 11 and over

Description of Project

Having had no success in setting up a reading group for teenagers, the Supervisor at Formby Library was interested in the success of Wargames events in libraries round the country, and decided to give them a try. The intention was to attract new users to the library.

In partnership with staff from the Games Workshop store, the first event was set up. The Games Workshop staff ran it, and brought all the items needed. All that the library had to do was advertise the event and provide refreshments. The store even provided prizes for a free draw.

Early in 2004, following enquiries from some of the participants, the library agreed to hold five more events with the possibility of setting up a Gaming Club. Free tickets were snapped up and there was a full house. The boys (so far it's been all boys) were so absorbed in painting or gaming that staff had to mimic a fanfare to get their attention for the free prize draw! For such a popular event it was very quiet and easy to run: there has been no conflict with regular users of the facilities.

The library has bought a selection of titles linked to the games so staff can mount more displays that will hopefully draw the gamers into reading as well as gaming. There is more information on the Games Workshop site: www.gamingclub.org.uk

Feedback from Library Staff

It was lovely to see the boys come in and enjoy the library – to see that this is a friendly place.
Library Supervisor

Project strengths

· The Games Workshop staff are helpful, both beforehand and on the day.
· The project addresses (indirectly) our LPSA target of increasing library usage by under-16 year-olds.

Weaknesses

· The event needs space – at least one table per activity
· Although initiallly facilitated by Games Workshop, a longer-term club would need to be organised by library staff (or volunteers)

Tips for other authorities wishing to repeat idea

· Talk to other authorities, to get 'inside information' on practicalities.
· If you plan to take photos, prepare a 'permission sheet', so parents/carers can sign in advance
· In order to attract the young people to reading, it's necessary to have a prominent display in the room so they can browse beforehand – once the event starts, all concentration is on the gaming!

Contact

Jenny Stanistreet,
Principal Library Services Officer (North)

jenny.stanistreet@leisure.sefton.gov.uk
Sefton MBC Leisure Services Dept
Pavilion Buildings
99-105 Lord Street
Southport, PR8 1RH
Tel: 0151 934 2351

Contact

Diana Ashcroft
Reader Development Librarian

diana.ashcroft@trafford.gov.uk
Coppice Library
Coppice Avenue
M33 4ND
Tel: 0161 912 3560

No Limits!
Trafford Metropolitan Borough Council across the authority
May 2003 onwards, targeting young people

Description of Project

In May of last year, Trafford Libraries launched a new collection of books specifically aimed at readers 13 and upwards – *No Limits!* The idea sprang from an earlier reading initiative – *Everybody's Reading* and the resultant selections made by the young people taking part in that project brought together teenage and adult books all of which appeal directly to young people. It is an ideal collection for the burgeoning and sometimes controversial genre of the crossover novel. For our adult readers it brings titles to their attention they may have missed and have since enjoyed like the *His Dark Materials* trilogy by Philip Pullman as well as the phenomenally popular *The Curious Incident of the Dog in the Night-Time* by Mark Haddon. But as Kate Kellaway (in *The Observer*, April 11 2004), points out: "What is not acknowledged though is that the traffic flows in the opposite direction – crossover fiction is also adult fiction that appeals to children". Witness then the success of Nick Hornby and Stephen King.

Our *No Limits!* collections, found in all of our libraries, also include books by less well-known writers but who all write about the feelings, concerns, hopes and the good things of being a young person today. The collections have more traditional reads – books which made an impact on society years ago but which are still relevant and true: *A Kestrel for a Knave* is just one example – there are many more.

CILIP acknowledges the benefits of promoting authors who write across age boundaries. The Carnegie website says: "This year's shortlist offers outstanding and immensely satisfying reading for anyone of 10 years and over, blurring the distinction between the traditionally separate genres of adult and children's books."

Project strengths

· Some of the barriers to borrowing books have now been removed so if a teenager wants to take out an adult book – they can do so: we think this helps to move reading choices from teenage to adult more easily.

· The promotion has been very popular – the collections are well-used and have attracted favourable comments.

· It complements our Adult and Children categories very well and we hope that we can develop and enhance the collections in the future.

Photo: Ian Lawson. The Three Graces, Liverpool
www.englandsnorthwest.com/

ICT creates a whole new world for reader development. The possibilities of two apparently competing areas of library service - books versus computers - working together is a hot issue at the moment and in the last couple of years, exciting, innovative approaches to this work have taken place on a national and regional level. A website called Book Forager began as a project for public libraries, pioneered by Opening The Book. In 2001, the New Opportunities Fund provided money to expand and rebrand the site as www.whichbook.net. This extremely user-friendly website demonstrates how the latest in database development helps people browse and choose books online. Opening The Book is about to launch a training package for frontline staff that would be delivered online via the library network.

Many of the national reading promotions such as World Book Day and *The Big Read* have road tested voting online via libraries as a way of engaging large audiences, and using the web to enable a local audience to interact with national authors. This new development should become less cumbersome as technology rises to meet the challenge (the World Book Day online festival had 1.4 million hits from 78 countries, double the figure for the previous year). In this region, the Time to Read web site **www.time-to-read.co.uk** enables professionals to share skills and information. Individually, library authorities have tested and designed web-based projects and sites that have a reader focus.

Anne Caldwell

Memories of Little Hulton

Salford City Council
Little Hulton Library, April-July 2004
Targeting older people who are isolated

Description of Project

This project followed on from a piece of work called *Stories of Salford* which helped local people to create stories with a story teller based on real stories in their particular areas. It also led on from basic skills work in this library.

Memories of Little Hulton is a series of learning opportunities related to old photos and stories of a particular area. Outcomes from the project include a website, a display and a booklet.

It has encouraged local people (young and old) to:

· Get involved in a local project
· Revisit their local library
· Learn new skills (ICT and basic skills where necessary)
· Create a record of one part of Salford
· Make new friends

The project was a joint piece of work between corporate ICT development workers, museums staff, basic skills providers, Age Concern and a range of library staff including the People's Network Manager, Reader Development Officer and Senior Librarian for Local Studies.

Feedback from Participants

I haven't seen Joyce for 20 years. If I hadn't come here today I would have just been sitting at home alone.

Some of these photos really bring back memories of things that I had forgotten.

It is good to create something for young people to read, so that they know that we had an interesting life too.

Project strengths

· Partnership working
· Easy to replicate in any local area
· Strong interest from the local community
· Creates a record that local people are interested in reading
· Website created: www.littlehultonmemories.colsal.org.uk
· Local history group created

Tips for other authorities wishing to repeat idea

· Ask for funding from your Lifelong Learning team.
· Ensure you have enough staff on hand to be able to break into small groups.
· Be aware of people with special needs (hearing loss, mobility problems etc).

Contact

Janet Swan
Reader Development Officer

janet.swan@salford.gov.uk
Eccles Library
Church Street
Eccles, M30 OEP
Tel: 0161 707 9612

Books to Go

Tameside Metropolitan Borough
Across the authority, 2004 onwards
Targeting people who are too busy to spend time in the library

Description of Project

Books to Go is an online service enabling customers to choose their books at the touch of a button! The service is aimed at people who are too busy to spend much time in the library, for example, parents with young children and people working long hours.

Tameside Libraries believe that this service was the first of its kind in the country and other authorities have since taken up the idea. By filling in a simple form readers can give an indication of the number and type of books they want and library staff do the rest, e-mailing or phoning when books are ready for collection at the library specified by the customer. It offers an opportunity to promote contemporary titles as well as more traditional material, as staff choose books based on readers' choices of genre.
Web site address: www.tameside.gov.uk/bookstogo

Project strengths

· Easy to manage
· Innovative – good for publicity
· Possibility for future growth of service

Weaknesses

· There has been a slow take-up
· Some early IT problems caused initial difficulties in e-mailing customers
· The site has received a large number of hits but this isn't reflected in use of the service

Tips for other authorities wishing to repeat idea

· Market the service with selected target groups,
· Make use of Council bulletin boards
· Service might be more successful in an authority with a high computer usage

Contact

Rachel Symonds
Social Inclusion Co-ordinator
Tameside Libraries

rachel.symonds@tameside.gov.uk
Heginbottom Mill
Old Street
Ashton-under-Lyne, OL6 7SG
Tel: 0161 342 2232

Oldham Readers and Writers Website

Oldham Metropolitan Borough Council
www.oldham.gov.uk/community/libraries/readers-writers
Launched September 2003, targeting IT users, readers and writers

oldh

www.oldham.gov.

Description of Project

The Readers and Writers website provides a means for people to find out about competitions, courses, groups and events. It gives people the chance to showcase their work on the *Works Online* section and to raise comments and questions with everything about reading and writing. From processing of user questions to linking in to major literary awards, the aim of the website is to provide easy use for all. There are plans to add a list of recommended books in Urdu and Bangla.

Divided into a section for readers and another for writers, it provides a clear and simple bridge from the literary to the technological. We want to use it to enhance the reading experience either through *Literary Links* or *Recommended Reading* or by providing a point of contact from a remote user to Oldham Libraries.

The site has recently been upgraded to make it content managed by library staff so that information can be sent live more quickly. This also gives us an opportunity to provide features to enable people to add book reviews and provide warnings on material that may be deemed offensive. We felt this was an important addition, which would enable us to include works that others may not wish to view. The new system makes it simpler for us to group *Works Online* into categories, i.e. into areas for poetry and stories for adults, and children's work. We can also highlight competitions and promotions we have carried out in libraries. It is also more interactive allowing comments to be added or responded to. The site has had nearly 70,000 hits to date.

Project strengths

· Far and away, the most used function is to submit work to the *Works Online* page. Not only does this enable writers to show off their work, it promotes Oldham as a place where literature is vibrant and relevant.

Weaknesses

· The main weakness of the project is that the website address is so long. It makes access to the site difficult. However, this is due to council policy of maintaining uniformity of access through the council website.

Tips for other authorities wishing to repeat idea

· We have found the support of the IT section invaluable. They have provided the structure and managed the content from the outset and have now designed a marvellous package which will enable us to maintain the website simply.

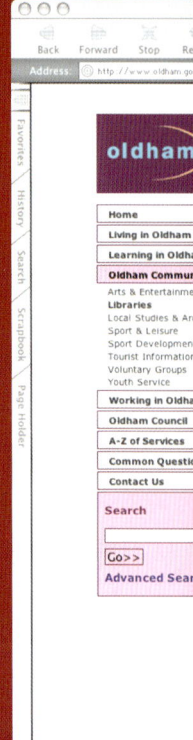

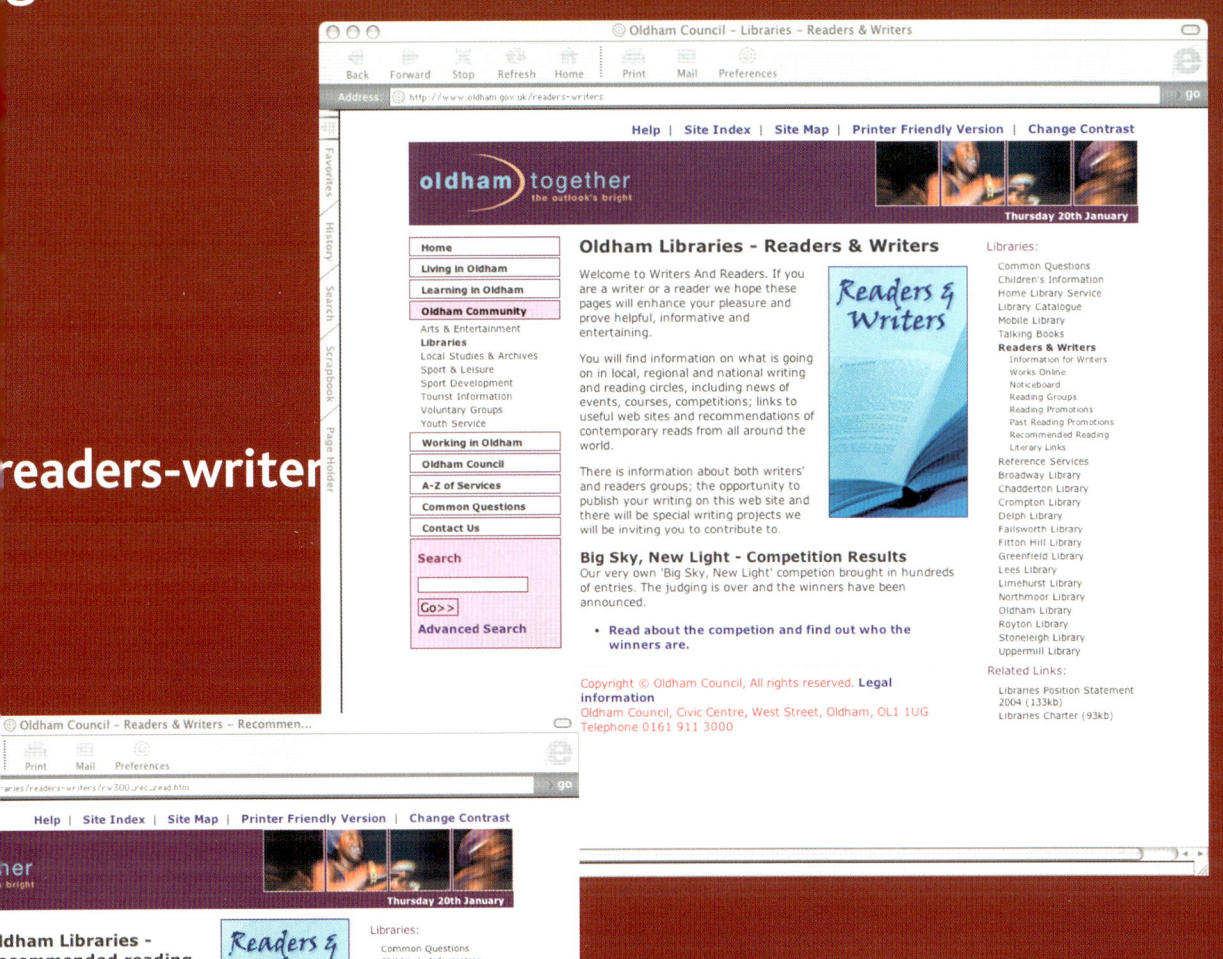

readers-writers

Contact

Helen Robinson
Literature Development Officer

helen.robinson@oldham.gov.uk
Oldham Library
Union Street
Oldham, OL1 1DN
Tel: 0161 911 4633

Photo: Ian Lawson. St. Helens Glass Museum
www.englandsnorthwest.com/

Until recent years, most traditional literature-based events and festivals would have the writer as a main focus of attention and assume that the audience would want little direct interaction other than asking a few questions at the end of a reading (and, of course, buying the author's books!). There have always been workshops aimed at writers improving their skills, or working alongside authors, but nothing aimed at readers. The picture has changed dramatically. *Opening The Book* pioneered the idea of making reading the focus of a cultural, public experience. Days of events dedicated towards readers were started in Bradford by the then development officer, Tom Palmer, and have now spread across the country. Many literature festivals include events for readers' groups and individuals to come together and interact with authors, and writers are now more frequently booked by libraries to talk about their reading, influences, and recommendations as well as their own work.

Funding bodies have also recognised this new development and have supported its growth. There will always be a place for readings, and, increasingly for spoken word and live literature events, but promoters and library staff are increasingly thinking of creative ways to engage readers. For example, the first Poetry Readers' Day took place in the North West of England in 2003 with an attendance of over sixty people. The poets who took part were very enthusiastic about the contact with an audience who had not only read their work, but also wanted to talk about reading poetry and their love of the art form.

Anne Caldwell

Poetry Readers' Day

Bury Met Theatre June 2003
Targeting members of North West library-based readers groups and the general public.

Description of Project

Manchester Poetry Festival was awarded funding from the Regional Arts Lottery Programme to hold a range of events in a wider area than Manchester City Centre. A Poetry Readers' day would fulfil the needs of both the Poetry Festival and the Time To Read network.

Poetry has a more limited appeal than the general readers' days that had successfully run in the region, but it was felt that it could also provide a training opportunity for library staff to find out more about poetry publishing and performers as well as for the general public to experience a poetry event outside Manchester city centre. The event was particularly promoted in and around Bury, but audience members did travel from further afield.

The day included the following:
· a poetry market, bookstalls from publishers, booksellers and poetry magazines
· opportunity to hear good readings from a diverse range of poets
· opportunity for 'local' writing and publishing groups to promote themselves to other poets and to library services
· opportunity for poets to recommend other poets they enjoy reading - readers' testimonies
· opportunity to discuss poems in a reading group setting
· information about poetry events and poetry collections in libraries

Over 60 people attended from a wide area. Poets involved on the day were Paul Farley, Sophie Hannah, Rommi Smith hosted by James Nash (below). Harry Owen, Cheshire's poet laureate, also took part, and four local poets had a reading spot at the end of the day.

Project strengths

· Funding partnership with Manchester Poetry Festival and input of their time on organisation.
· Enthusiasm of poets taking part in a readers' day for the first time.

Weaknesses

· Indifferent support from some publishers.
· Some problems with venue. There can often be difficulties when you don't control the venue directly.

Tips for other authorities wishing to repeat idea

· Start organising very early.
· Talk to the poets about aims for the day and be precise about what you want them to do.
· Get lots of staff involved - to talk up the day with potential audience members, and to help at the event.

Feedback from participant

A real learning day for me. I feel a better person after today than I started. I'm so glad I came.

Contact

Jane Mathieson
Time to Read Co-ordinator

nwreader@libraries.manchester.gov.uk
c/o Manchester Central Library
St Peter's Square
Manchester
M2 5PD
Tel: 0161 236 4451

A Taste of Verse and Poetry Party in the Palm House
Liverpool City Council
Liverpool Central Library, National Poetry Day 2003 and Sefton Park
Targeting the general public

Description of Project

These two events were run as part of National Poetry Day celebrations in the city. Liverpool Libraries and Information Services hosted a *Taste of Verse* event at lunch time in the Central Library for people hungry for poetry. The public were invited to come along to hear their favourite poems read and were reminded not to forget their sandwiches. Over 60 attended and plenty brought along a poem to read, including the Director of Education, Library and Sports Services, Colin Hilton, and the Head of Libraries and Information Services, Joyce Little. Several people asked for requests but could not remember the author or the correct title of their favourite poem. This tested the knowledge of staff and poetry resources of the library to the full, all requests were identified and read. Thank goodness for the Internet!
The event was ably hosted by Jane Davis of *The Reader* Magazine.

Poetry Party in the Palm House

The *Taste of Verse* event was twinned with a **Poetry Party in the Palm House**, Sefton Park on Sunday 12th October. The public were invited to listen to Liverpool's favourite poems amongst the palms and hear their poetry requests read aloud. Book stalls were set up, prizes and giveaways were distributed, there were activities for kids and everyone enjoyed the festive party atmosphere.

The take up was amazing! Dozens of people came forward to read their favourite poems and several performed their own work. A wide range of poems was performed by a diverse range of performers! Demand exceeded the time available and all the tact of the MC was needed to organise the performers. The audience soared to more than 300. Some stayed for the full session, others moved on. Altogether the event proved a triumph and proved there is an audience for poetry.

Project strengths

· A simple idea – cheap and easy to arrange
· The Palm House readings reached new audiences for poetry and libraries

Tips for other authorities wanting to repeat the idea

· Use a venue with character: the Palm House was ideal.

Contact

Ron Travis
Manager, Community Libraries

ron.travis@liverpool.gov.uk
Liverpool Central Library
William Brown St
Liverpool
L3 8EW
Tel: 0151 233 5847

Reading The Games

Manchester City Council
Reading Festival tied in with Commonwealth Games 2002
Libraries across Manchester- May – July 2002
Targeting library users, school age children, the general public

Contact

Jane Mathieson
Time to Read Co-ordinator

nwreader@libraries.manchester.gov.u
c/o Manchester Central Library
St Peter's Square
Manchester,
M2 5PD
Tel: 0161 236 4451

Description of Project

This reading festival aimed to promote Commonwealth writers and to encourage library users to read material from the Commonwealth. It was to have a wide appeal and attract a culturally diverse audience to events. The festival complemented the games themselves and took cultural activity into distant suburbs of the city, and into smaller, community libraries.

20 events were organised, featuring novelists, storytellers, poets and performers from four continents. They took the form of free public events, schools events by invitation and workshops for local writers. Our monthly poetry readings in Central Library featured Commonwealth poets and a day-long Asian Literature and Arts Festival took place in Longsight. We also created and promoted a Games-themed Summer Reading Game, encouraging children to make use of their libraries during the summer holidays, and a booklist of Commonwealth writing. The Library service worked in partnership with the Literatures of the Commonwealth Festival (the first major literature festival ever held in Manchester), the Festival of Manchester Writing and publishers Commonword to deliver a diverse and interesting range of writers, designed to appeal to the widest possible audience. All but one of the events were free.

· 1,200 people visited the events in libraries and the service benefited greatly from increased publicity through the wider Cultureshock arts festival listings.

· The library service's participation in this event and the quality of the print produced greatly enhanced the service's standing and reputation within the literary and educational community in the city. The brochure received a CILIP publicity award in 2003.

· Valuable links were created with the Urdu-speaking community in Longsight as a result of the Asian Literature and Arts Festival.

· Work for 32 writers, musicians and performers.

Feedback from library staff and participants

The quality of the print and promotion and the especially good prizes for the reading game certainly got children involved.
Staff quote

I liked the way (he) brought the poems to life. I never liked poetry at school
From one of the poetry readings

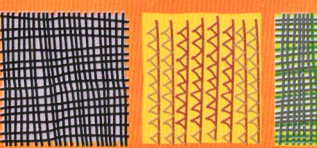

manchester librarie

reading
the Games

a programme of events to celebrate the Commonwealth Game

Project strengths

· Quality of print publicity was excellent – probably the best we have ever done.

· It brought a range of new young black writers into libraries - good for us to discover them and has led to follow-on events with several of them

· Getting support from a publisher was helpful - we booked five Black Amber writers who were all excellent.

· It took the cultures of the Commonwealth into suburbs otherwise untouched by the Games.

Weaknesses

· The aim of putting writers into libraries with no previous history of events of any sort was too risky. Very poor audiences for one or two writers. This needed much more outreach work.

· The Manchester Metropolitan University-based *Literatures of the Commonwealth Festival* did clash with one of our events, but a partnership with them also enhanced both programmes.

Tips for other authorities wishing to repeat idea

· Tying in with a high profile cultural festival is very exciting and brings new promotional opportunities.

· You need to use the opportunity to promote the library service – particularly its role in reaching a wide, community-based audience that may not see a City-Centre Festival as being "for them"

Words '04: Literature Festival

Leigh and Wigan Words Together – Wigan Local Authority.
Leigh Library and Wigan Venues April 14th-17th 2004
Targeting anyone with an interest in words, plus children/families, asylum and refugee communities and recovering patients

Description of Project

Words 04 was a community literature festival combining reading, writing and performance and a collaboration between many individuals and organisations: Wigan Leisure and Culture Trust, Libraries, Wigan and Leigh College; Towpath Community Press; Wigan Pier Theatre Company; many writers' groups from around the Borough; Leigh's Bookchat reading group and others.

The festival was a rich mix of plays, poetry, novels, stand-up; of workshops, performances, readings and talks; of competitions and chances to participate. Highlights at Leigh included Tony Warren, the creator of *Coronation Street* (whose frank and very funny talk was rated by one visitor as *'the best afternoon I've had since Christmas!')* and crime writer Margaret Murphy with a fascinating exploration of research methods for crime novelists. There was a hilarious if over-long community play evening and a touching and inspiring session on *Writing on the Way to Recovery* in which patients recovering from depression and mental illness described how creative writing had helped and inspired them. A vibrant writers' marketplace was held, where publishers and local groups showcased their work, and an immensely practical question and answer session on the art of writing and getting published with scriptwriter Paul Finch. Manchester poet Mandy Coe led a workshop/performance session for members of refugee/asylum communities, and two performance sessions were well attended and lively.
Over four days (Wednesday to Saturday) more than 700 people attended 18 events: evaluations were 80% excellent or good. There is a strong demand for another festival and *Words '05* is being planned.

Feedback from audience

We had so much fun at Words '04 and we're hoping to be there next year!
Comments on the day showed how much people were enjoying the events and how surprised they were at the amount of things going on... you can give yourselves a pat on the back on the excellent programme...
Cait Myers, BeWrite.net

Contact

Stephen Lythgoe
Reader in Residence, Wigan

s.lythgoe@wlct.org
Leigh Library
Civic Square
Leigh
WNT 1EB
Tel: 01942 404 566

Project strengths

· The large committee, drawn from several organisations, ensured a balanced programme. However the size and scattered locations of the participants made decision making difficult.

Weaknesses

· Despite a lot of effort, local news coverage was patchy at best; and the press, although invited to everything, did not cover one event. Why wasn't it news?

· On reflection we tried to do too much in too short a time: an extra day to spread events into would have been better.

· The audience we got came mainly from the "traditional" library demographic (mainly white; 40+ women and 50+ retired men): cause for concern for next time, though events were pretty much fully booked.

Tips for other authorities wishing to repeat idea

· You need lots of time and energy and a strong and well balanced committee: the festival was a community event with strong library participation, not just a library initiative.

· A mix of events to cater for writers, readers, and performers is needed to create widespread interest: not just a writing group jamboree.

· A couple of big names will generate most of the pre-publicity while a local connection may draw the biggest audiences.

· Include children's and family events and get schools involved.

· Well-designed and printed publicity is essential.

eigh & Wigan Words Together First

WIGAN LEISURE & CULTURE TRUST IN PARTNERSHIP WITH

north west Playwrights

ll was destined to a barren stra
y fortress, and a dubious hand;
t the name, at which the world g
nt a mortal, or adorn a tale.

Description of Project

Trafford Libraries held its very first Readers' Day in 2004. Our intention was to present a programme of activities, workshops and talks that would appeal to the whole family. We also had in mind a number of themes to underpin the event which we hoped would enhance people's enjoyment of the different sessions. These themes could also provide a focus for the writers and performers as to how to construct their sessions.

As the writer Dodie Smith once lived in the area, we asked her biographer to come and give us a talk on her life and work. Her book *101 Dalmatians* provided the idea for a story-sack which was later given as a prize at one of the early activity sessions. Her *I Capture the Castle* is a title that can be perceived as a crossover novel which was a theme we wished to explore in more depth. We invited four locally-based writers who justifiably fulfilled the criteria – Sherry Ashworth, Adèle Geras, , Melvin Burgess and Paul Magrs (pictured opposite) to help us to do that. We also booked the well-known illustrator Tony Ross; and The Storyteller. As it was the start of Euro 2004, Craig Bradley used football to attract boys and their fathers to join some fast-paced activities.

Feedback from participants

Lovely – more please!
Very enjoyable with plenty of ideas to try at home
Excellent entertainment – spellbinding stories
I attended sessions with Tony Ross and 'The Storyteller' with my daughter and the author panel discussion on my own. It inspired me to continue exploring the rich world of books, stories and reading at all levels and to do what I can as a parent and teaching assistant to encourage others to do the same.

Project strengths

· The staff who were involved on the day enjoyed it enormously.

· For those who had not been to a Readers' Day before it was a very pleasant surprise – they felt that they could enthuse other colleagues for any similar events we may hold in the future.

· We were able to work with other departments and it certainly raised our profile within the council.

Weaknesses

· The turn out was lower than we wanted

· Had we tried to appeal to too large an audience?

· Maybe it just didn't capture the imagination?

· Unfortunately the publicity was delayed and didn't give us that long in which to promote the day.

...na Ashcroft
...der Development Librarian

...a.ashcroft@trafford.gov.uk
...pice Library
...pice Avenue
...3 4ND
...0161 912 3560

Tips for other authorities wishing to repeat idea

· It was essential to hold a debriefing session to look at participants' comments and evaluation sheets.

Photo: Courtesy of Trafford Libraries

Festive Readers' Day

Wirral Libraries
Thursday 4th December 2003
Targeting library reading groups and people interested in reading or joining a group

Description of Project

We wanted to celebrate the growing success of our Library reading groups and put on a festive event which brought together library staff, readers and the community in a light hearted atmosphere.
We decided on a library venue with a public hall attached and decorated and adorned the room with book displays, author profiles, books and poinsettias (as instead of 30, our parks department delivered 300). Children from the local school opened the event by singing a selection of Christmas carols, a classical guitarist played Christmas music, books were offered for sale by a local bookseller and author sessions were arranged throughout the afternoon and evening.

Small rooms were available for the author talks; quizzes, mince pies and mulled wine provided the backdrop. Authors Clare Dudman and Margaret Murphy joined our local historian Ralph Brocklebank and poet Gladys Mary Coles in making this a very special and successful event. It had been organised on a shoe-string budget and in the end we had an audience of over 100 with numerous library staff supporting and bringing along their reading groups. We will do it again.

Feedback from borrowers and staff

Great evening, lots of activity but needs to be in every library.
Staff thought it was a great opportunity to get back to books.

Project strengths

· Staff enthusiasm and energy, great joint opportunity where reading groups welcomed the chance to meet other readers

Project Weaknesses

· Not enough funding: we will need to look for sponsorship in the future.
· Some of the author talks were too long; they needed to be more specific and more able to control the timing.

Tips for other authorities wishing to repeat idea

· Timing is essential, good communication with the speakers and lots of staff support.

Contact

Sue Powell
Area Librarian South

suepowell@wirral-libraries.net
Bebington Central Library
Civic Way
Bebington
Wirral CH63 7PN
Tel: 0151 643 7222

Joint Readers' Days

March 13th 2004 Stockport & Tameside
May 21st 2004 Oldham & Rochdale
Targeting readers and library users, in particular readers' group members

Description of Project

One of the aims of the Time To Read partnership in 2002 was to secure funding for a number of Readers' Days across the NW region. A bid was made to the Arts Council England, NW for funding for a minimum of five days to be held in different parts of the region. The intention was that a range of models for future activity was tested. Funding was obtained and the first two days were joint events, heavily marketed and promoted in neighbouring authorities, as well as sharing organisation, staffing and match funding commitment.

Time to Read wanted to test partnership planning and delivery, to share the workload and provide days for a wide group of readers. Time to Read was also interested to see if significant numbers of readers were prepared to travel to a neighbouring authority.

Feedback from participant

This is an excellent way of bringing a large and varied number of readers together socially

Project strengths

· Sharing resources means more is achievable
· More staff to help in advance and on the day
· Staff meet each other from neighbouring authorities - more awareness of each others' services
· More potential audience
· Broadens the horizons of library users
· More funding towards publicity costs

Project Weaknesses

· Where to hold the event is a dilemma. It needs stronger marketing in the neighbouring authority.
· The partnership approach was not entirely successful. It is unusual to be asked to promote something outside your own authority.

Tips for other authorities wishing to repeat idea

· Start talking as early as possible.
· Share the workload as much as possible.
· See Reader's Day Toolkit at www.time-to-read-co.uk

Contact

Jane Mathieson
Time to Read Co-ordinator

nwreader@libraries.manchester.gov.uk
c/o Manchester Central Library
St Peter's Square
Manchester
M2 5PD
Tel: 0161 236 4451

Photo: Ian Lawson. Lake Windermere, Cumbria
www.englandsnorthwest.com/

A renaissance is taking place in many library buildings. As the original fixtures and fittings of our public spaces wear out, programmes of refurbishment are giving an opportunity for library staff to consider the function and use of the building in new ways. Lessons have been taken from the retail trade and from the American author Paco Underhill's writing (*Why We Buy*) on the psychology of how people use spaces. Many new library refurbishments have used *Opening The Book*'s applications of this work and employed the company as consultants. The company has designed its own range of display furniture.

At the same time, library suppliers of fixtures and fittings have listened to what the sector requires and been willing to experiment with new ways of displaying books in a reader-friendly manner. The big shift in thinking that has taken place echoes the progress in other areas of reader development work, which is to place the customer at the centre of the service, consider their needs, and how our buildings can work for them to encourage reading.

Anne Caldwell

Tracking Surveys

Warrington Local Authority
Warrington Library, Padgate, Birchwood and Westbrook Library, July 2002

Description of Project

An exercise designed by *Opening The Book* to track how customers use library spaces formed the basis for a piece of research run in Warrington Libraries in 2002. It involved observing and recording how customers used the library space over a period of time, noting lengths of visits, whether people borrowed material, where they went and the profile of who was using the library. The main findings were as follows:

· Average visit length was 4-8 minutes, and for young people as little as 75 seconds!
· Between 48% and 63% of library users do not borrow anything
· The people who do visit briefly borrow the most, i.e. are purposeful
· Large print, teenage and careers sections of stock were the least popular.

We highlighted the following main problems:

· Poor external signing
· Security systems and gates acting as barriers to browsing
· Crowded rows of stock – difficult for quick browsers to choose
· One corner was an unattractive dumping ground for old furniture
· Books all shelved spine on, even promotions
· No posters or face-on displays
· Entrance areas and counters very cluttered
· Prime space used for book sales

Following these results, we also did the tracking exercise in other libraries where use had significantly declined. As a result, Westbrook library was refurbished, and the survey results were used to determine a new layout. Adult fiction issues dipped in the first year, but there was a 20.5% increase in non-fiction. Junior issues rose by 12%.

What did we do?
· Moved the new book display stand to be the first thing people see
· Relocated items for sale into dead zones and used prime space to promote books
· Took notices from pillars and windows and put them on notice boards
· Front-faced all promotional material and the *Just Returned* area.
· Created staff recommendations shelves and areas for themed book displays
· Informed staff about changes and encouraged them to put material face-on

Contact

Fiona Barry
Principal libraries Manager

f.barry@warrington.gov.uk
Warrington Central Library
Museum Street
Warrington, WA1 1JB
Tel: 01925 442 889

Book Buffet

Knowsley Local Authority

Knowsley Libraries 2001 – targeting adult browsers

Description of Project

This project began as a tabletop display of books recommended by staff. Over ninety titles were suggested by staff in all the branches. The list was edited to twenty-five titles and these were arranged into a reading menu. There were 'starters' to whet the appetite, heavier 'main courses' to get your teeth into, and 'desserts' for something light to finish. Each library had three copies of each title and a book list in the form of a menu was printed.

Feedback from customer

These were mouthwatering books to satisfy your appetite for a good read!

Project strengths

· Staff knew the books and were able to promote them
· The food theme was popular

Weaknesses

· A lot of time was needed for staff consultation

Tips for other authorities wishing to repeat idea

· Include staff from the beginning and use money to produce a professional book list

BOOK BUFFET

Treat yourself from our tempting, tasty titles recommended by staff

Contact

Sue Stone
Reading Co-ordinator

sue.stone.dlcs@knowsley.gov.uk
Stockbridge Library
The Withens
Stockbridge Village
Liverpool, L28 1SU
Tel: 0151 443 5001

Description of Project

This idea developed from a conversation with Paul Bellard, of Spectrum Sign & Display Ltd., when he was measuring up our libraries for People's Network signage. We commented that we had not come across a display stand that was compact, stylish, lightweight and, most important of all, inexpensive. Spectrum works in acrylics, so it should have been possible to design something to suit. As a trial we were promised a foam board prototype. Mk.1 duly arrived. Literally and metaphorically we pulled it apart. Undeterred, Paul made further sketches, asked more questions and went away. Some weeks later, Mk.2 arrived. It was lightweight, the clear acrylic top slotted neatly into the fibreboard base, there were four display shelves and a top panel for a poster. We put it to the test.

Project strengths

• It looked good
• A small enough "footprint" to be positioned at the end of shelving units
• Borrowers were attracted to it and staff found it an asset for "instant" display.

Weaknesses

• The shelves did not sustain the weight of books,
• It was difficult to insert/extract the poster
• The staff bumped into the stand

Result ...finally, Paul presented us with Mk.3. This features a brushed acrylic effect for greater visibility, thumb-holes for poster access, and a much sturdier shelf design. We bought them for all our branches and, because they have been so successful, have placed repeat orders.

Tips for other authorities wishing to repeat idea
• Think hard about both user and staff requirements.

Contact

Jenny Stanistreet
Principal Library Services Officer (North)

Sefton MBC Leisure Services Dept
jenny.stanistreet@leisure.sefton.gov.uk
Pavilion Buildings
99-105 Lord Street
Southport PR8 1RH
Tel: 0151 934 2351

Reader-centred Displays
Lancashire County Council
All 84 static libraries, targeting browsers, in particular the 16 to 35 age range. 2003 onwards.

Description of Project

As part of the Reader Development Strategy, reader-centred displays were introduced to all libraries across Lancashire. Our aim was to create attractive and stimulating displays to appeal to browsers and which would require a minimal amount of maintenance from staff.

A number of themed collections were created consisting of attractive looking fiction and non-fiction paperbacks, as well as DVDs, videos and CDs. These included:

• *Route 66* (read your way across America)
• *Cutting Edge* (First crime novels)
• *Destinations* (Travel Writing)
• *Red Rose Reading* (Reading Group recommendations)
• *Rush Hour* (Short Stories)
• *Unfocused* (All that non-fiction stock that is really cool but gets lost in the Dewey sequence)

Initial stock was ordered in multiple copies. No collection is based on a specific list, so they can be topped up during the standard book selection process, or as a result of borrower feedback. Collections are made up of around 80 items but more are included when sent to larger libraries.
Furniture was commissioned from Norseman who designed and built display bins to our specification. Feedback forms *Writeback* have been introduced for the public, to enable staff to assess the impact of the displays and gather ideas for future collections.
Collections are based in libraries for two months to create maximum impact. During the third month, as the collection is gathered in to send to another branch, the library puts together its own display. This has the benefit of allowing staff to put into practice their training and ideas.

Feedback from borrowers

I'm confident about the quality of material selected...I feel safe in the knowledge I can grab something when I'm in a hurry and know that it will stimulate and please.
I loved this book so much I've borrowed it twice now

Project strengths

• Borrowers see, use and appreciate a constantly changing variety of promotions which are adaptable to the needs of a particular library.
• Libraries have good quality display furniture they can adapt for specific one-off promotions.
• Collections are easily maintained.

Weaknesses

• Time taken in preparing initial collections

Tips for other authorities wishing to repeat idea

• Check out prices of furniture – it's not too expensive to have something custom made

Contact

Alison Thies
Service Development Officer

alison.thies@lcl.lancss.gov.uk
c/o Room D21
Lancashire County Council
County Hall, Fishergate
Preston PR1 8XJ
Tel: 01772 534051

Description of Project

The Breakout Area is a specific area of the library for young people above the age of eleven. Previously, the space for young adults was small, and dominated by picture books. This discouraged older teenagers from using the collection.

The Breakout Area stock is drawn from all parts of the library and includes some adult fiction and non fiction, CDs, videos and graphic novels. We looked for subjects that we thought would interest the target age group such as art, music, books on issues, horror, fantasy fiction, tattooing and body decoration. The single most popular book currently is Darren Shann's *Cirque du Freak*.

Project strengths

• We avoided the term 'teenage area'
• We now have some magnificent art work in this area of the library

Tips for authorities wishing to repeat idea

• We felt that by appealing to the age group and letting them discover the *Breakout Area* for themselves they would feel more at home.
• The books are shelved informally by interest group.
• We are still experimenting and will add art work and continue to improve the focus of the area.

Contact

Paul Marland
Prinicipal Libraries Manager

paul.marland@blackpool.gov.uk
Leisure, Culture & Community Learning
c/o P.O. Box 77
Town Hall
Blackpool, FY1 1AD
Tel: 01253 478112

Description of Project

The aim was to increase use of the library. After national and local research into how design and layout can be improved, the changes we made included:
- Creating a browsing area and sociable spaces with sofas to relax and read
- Creating a quick choice selection to facilitate the 5-10 minute visitor
- Enlarging the available space for the children making it vibrant and colourful
- Incorporating good practice from the retail sector, using forward-facing and tabletop display
- Introducing three small customer service points where library procedures are carried out.
  One is lower to facilitate access for children and people with disabilities.
- Furniture wherever possible is on wheels so that library space is flexible.
- Developing a marketing strategy to entice non-users and occasional users.

Importantly we involved the staff in the consultation process right from the very beginning. Staff were provided with training so that they understood the concepts behind what we were trying to achieve and could continue making the library visually appealing once it had re-opened.

We targeted in particular 16-25 year olds, parents and carers of children 0-9, Young people 10-15 and 5-10 minute borrowers.

Feedback from customers

A real show stopper! It looks wonderful and very inviting - will the readers ever leave?

Junior is a dream with games available!!!!! You rebels. Well done.

It's like being in a bookshop. All we need now is a coffee machine.

Project strengths
- Overwhelmingly positive response from the customers and staff.
- Many staff from other authorities have been to look, with a view to undertaking similar projects
- Increased use of junior library and the extra space available has meant we could start a successful Family Reading group.

Weaknesses
- Very small budget
- Short timescale in which to complete the project

Tips for other authorities wishing to repeat idea
- Start the consultation process as early as possible.
- Get a scale drawing of the library and look at it as an empty shell. Don't be constrained by what is already in place.
- Talk to local joinery firms. They can often produce bespoke furniture to exact requirements, competitively priced.
- Continue to promote the project after it has been completed.

Contact

Jane Evans
Senior Libraries Manager

jane.evans@stockport.gov.uk
Phoenix House
Birdhall Lane
Cheadle Heath, Stockport
SK3 0RA
Tel. 0161 474 5751

78

Photo: Ian Lawson. Rochdale Town Hall
www.englandsnorthwest.com/

Since the 2000 report *Open to All,* the contribution libraries make to tackle social exclusion has been highlighted and is high on current government agendas.

Many library services in the North West of England have a strong tradition of trying to provide inclusive services. In recent years projects engaged in by Time to Read (Listen 'Ear, Reading Lifelines, Everybody's Reading) have all been aimed at potentially excluded people. There is also an overlap between reader development and work to support literacy, and authorities in the region have been involved with The Reading Agency's *Vital Link* project, or bought into its materials.

The *YouthBoox* project coordinated by The Reading Agency highlighted the positive benefits of youth workers and library staff working together to tackle social inequalities, particularly with young people. The document *Fulfilling Their Potential,* June 2004 (led by The Reading Agency with contributions from librarians as part of the Framework for the Future Action Plan) encourages libraries to be more responsive to young people's needs in designing services, and more dynamic in their delivery and marketing.

Anne Caldwell

BRAIN: Bury Reading and Information Network

Bury Metropolitan Borough Council
Outreach Project. Commenced 2003 – ongoing
Targeting young people experiencing social exclusion and their families

Description of Project

The project involves
· Encouraging reading for leisure and information
· Use of online information sources and increasing IT skills
· Art activities
· Creative writing
· Developing library collections with and for the community to reflect diverse cultural backgrounds
· Encouraging children and families to read and learn together
· Improving the skills of parents in areas such as story telling and encouraging reading
· Training Library staff and others in more effective ways of helping 5-13 year olds

Sample activities:
South Cross St Garden

This project was based at a library housed in a multi-use community centre in a predominantly Asian area, in partnership with SRB and the local Tenants and Residents Association. Local residents of all ages submitted designs for a garden and children, under the guidance of library staff and a community artist, have since been involved in reading, art and storytelling sessions about gardens and nature, using books and the internet for inspiration. The major outcome is a mural on the garden wall which the children painted, together with community artist Tina Foran. The project has been a tremendous success, with participants thoroughly enjoying themselves while learning skills such as negotiation and teamwork.

Big Read Inter-generational reading project

A reading event held at a Day Care Centre for the elderly. Children from Years Four and Five of a local school chose four favourite books from the BBC Top 100 books. Each child produced a report on their favourite title; later included in a display of children's work in Bury Central Library. Episodes from the book were dramatised and performed for centre users. The users of the centre discussed their favourite books with the children. The children also made puppets to represent characters from the books. The event was attended by the Mayor and received coverage in the local press.

The Big Draw

Working in partnership with Life Long Learning, BRAIN commissioned two community artists to develop a joint reading and drawing project to contribute to the national *Big Draw* event. The day was delivered in English and Urdu and was attended by 95 children and 23 adults.   Approximately 30% of participants were from the Asian community. Activities included storytelling and group discussion on the day's chosen topics of the animal kingdom, the environment and recycling. A large collage inspired by the book *The Tin Forest* was produced by the children and was on display in Bury Art Gallery for two months.

Feedback from participants and supporters

BRAIN is making a tremendous difference to the whole school. Children are really enthused, not only by the special projects, but also by the follow-up work we carry out.   Children who previously showed little interest in reading are starting to enjoy books for the first time.
Head of a primary school

BRAIN is the best thing in the world; I want Jean to come every day and make lots of things with us.
7 year old boy at South Cross Street

My friends laughed when I said I was taking part in the project but when I told them what I had been doing they wanted to come as well. **13 year old girl**

Project strengths

· Flexibility - we have been able to adapt the project to suit demand and the developing needs of children
· A fairly generous budget for events and materials which can be spent more or less as we see fit
· Established contacts to get the project up and running and from them have developed new ones
· Well designed publicity materials
· Managerial and political support - we have made sure local councillors know what is going on and invited them to events
· Partnerships - working with other agencies such as SRBs and residents groups to extend the project and bring in more funding
· Excellent working relationship with the funding body - we are currently working with them to produce a newsletter for all the projects in the area

Weaknesses

Needs to be a full-time project!

Tips for other authorities wishing to repeat idea

· Make friends with your funders - don't just think about what they can do for you, look for what you can do for them - doing this led to additional support.
· Ensure your project is enjoyable for all concerned including the adults - even the most worthy project will not succeed if no one enjoys it.
· Don't be afraid to blow your own trumpet.
· Listen to the children - they have so many good ideas and they will spread the good news for you.
· Look at other agencies - can you link in with them to extend/improve what you are doing?
· Record everything - particularly with photographs and let people see them.

Contact

Jean Lonsdale
Library Outreach Worker

j.lonsdale@bury.gov.uk
Social Inclusion Unit
Bury Central Library
Manchester Road
Bury, BL9 0DG
Tel: 0161 253 6104

Description of Project

Families Reading Together was a project funded by Neighbourhood Renewal in the West Sutton area of St Helens. It aimed to raise the profile of reading as a life long, enjoyable activity within families and the profile of Chester Lane library. St Helens Libraries managed the project with a large input from the Family Learning section of the council. Reading groups were run in schools, the local sheltered housing complex and in the library. A weekly story time for pre-school children was set up at the library and story times were also held in Sure Start playgroups. ICT courses and taster sessions ran in the library, schools and other community venues. Accredited course such as *Supporting Early Reading* were held, and schools were given funds to buy *Curiosity Kits* and other supporting material. Arts sessions where parents were encouraged to have a go alongside their kids were very popular, as were competitions and quizzes in the library to tie in to national events such as World Book Day.

A number of one-off events showed the creative ways that families could read together:

• *It's Magic* – a dance/creative play session linked to Roald Dahl's *The Witches*

• *Five Minutes' Peace* – a pampering session to complement the launch of a selection of books for mums and carers of young children

• Visits by children's authors to schools and the library including Bob Wilson, Peter Carey, Dennis Bond and Alan Gibbons

CD-ROMs, new books, a web site and interactive white board were installed at the library for use by the community and local groups. From April 2004, the project was renamed *Families Learning Together* and has moved to Parr Library, to continue the successful work done at West Sutton.

Photo: Karen Wright

Contact

Carol Booth
Reader Development Worker

carol.booth@merseymail.com
c/o Parr Library
Fleet Lane,
St Helens, WA9 1SY
Tel: 01744 678704

Description of Project

Knowsley Library Service was one of the nine library authorities involved in the pilot phase of *The Vital Link*, a DCMS / Wolfson Public Libraries Challenge funded project which ran during 2001/2002. The pilot aimed to develop links between libraries and basic skills providers through reader development targeted at adults with literacy needs. It brought together a real partnership of library and literacy organisations to create models of good practice to inspire, support and motivate emergent adult readers. In Knowsley, strong links were formed between the Library Service and Knowsley Community College's Adult and Community Education Department (ACE). Knowsley had been identified by the Basic Skills Agency as having an above average percentage of people in the post-16 age bracket with literacy needs. Within the Borough, Page Moss and Stockbridge Village were identified as areas of particular need. Activities, ranging from a creative writers' group through to sessions with basic skills students, were initiated and sustained.

One group targeted by *The Vital Link* was the Mother and Toddler group that meets at Stockbridge Village Community Centre, next door to the library. This group of young mothers and carers had been involved in discussion sessions around reading. Consultation revealed that parents and carers tended not to make return visits to the library and community centre after dropping older children at school and attending the playgroup: carers felt that they didn't have enough time to spend choosing books for themselves. To remedy this, a bulk loan to the group from the library was arranged so that carers could choose their reading materials during their sessions in the community centre.

A pamper morning was arranged as a vehicle to launch the scheme. Knowsley Community College ACE was invited to provide a quiz around skin care, and then sessions in facial massage, cleansing and toning. They talked to the group about learning opportunities with the college. Avenues for promotion of the event included the local health centre, The Villages Housing Trust and the community centre.

Project Strengths

· It was a targeted audience: although open to the general public,
  the main focus was the mother and toddler group;
· The timing and location was convenient for the group.
· The group was consulted about what activities they would be interested in.
· The event was publicised locally, through posters, flyers, the local
  community newspaper and, most importantly, word of mouth.
· The event had committed support from both
  the Library and college staff.

Contact

Sue Stone

Reading Co-ordinator
sue.stone@knowsley.gov.uk
Stockbridge Library
The Withins
Stockbridge Village
Knowsley, L28 1SU
Tel: 0151 443 5001

Brooker Centre Bibliotherapy Project

Halton Borough Council
April 2003 – continuing, targeting patients

Description of Project

Heath Ward is a mixed hospital ward for those aged 65 years and older who suffer from a functional mental illness. The average length of stay in hospital is no more than four to six weeks.
Sessions run weekly in the centre and during each session extracts are read from books and poems around a theme, patients are encouraged to talk about what they had heard and share the memories these evoked for them. The themes include Childhood Memories, Schooldays, Travel, Humour, Wartime and The Day War broke out. Books and poems are selected from library stock and supplemented by Internet sources. Large Print handouts of song lyrics or poems are produced for each session.

Project strengths

· The emphasis is not on people reading books for themselves, but on being able to enjoy books through listening and sharing their responses with a small group. Therefore visually impaired people and people suffering from dementia are able to take part and enjoy books.
· The reading group sessions provide a mentally stimulating activity and generate new topics of conversation.
· Taking part in a reading group session helps people get to know each other.
· People derive great pleasure from taking part in a small group activity, where their views are listened to and they can feel valued. This in turn helps the development of communication skills, and can help to raise people's self-esteem and improve self-confidence.
· The groups encourage self-expression and the sharing of thoughts, memories and personal experiences with other people.
· A book collection, consisting of large print titles and talking books, has been placed in the day room for patients' use. Ward staff also use the collection when working on a one-to-one basis with certain patients.

Weaknesses

· Success of a session depends on clients' participation. Sometimes, due to the nature of the medical conditions, they cannot or do not want to become involved.
· Needs support of hospital staff.
· Can be quite emotionally draining for the person conducting the session.

Tips for other authorities wishing to repeat idea

· Approach local services such as hospitals.
· Ideally six sessions is long enough to assess as to whether or not it is going to be successful.

Contact

Janette Fleming
Reader Development Officer

janette.fleming@halton-borough.gov.uk
Halton Lea Library
Runcorn
WA7 2PF
Tel: 01928 715351

Family Literacy Project

Cumbria County Council
Cumbria November 2003 – ongoing
Targeting young people under 19, adults with literacy needs, and families across the county

Description of Project

Three community development workers have led this project since November 2003. They have built great links within their communities, promoting the library service and working with the libraries' Young People's team. One successful strand of work has been called *Telling Tales Together* – in partnership with Adult Education. The work involved rolling out a series of fifteen-week storytelling courses held in libraries. Courses generated 189 enrolments across the county.

They were backed up with the purchase of the *First Choice* book promotion aimed at adults with basic skills needs. Plans are now underway to roll out another set of courses called *Rhyme Time*, which would be accredited. The courses cover topics such as the history of nursery rhymes, rhymes from childhood and the playground, action rhymes and number rhymes. Stock from this field has been purchased to support libraries hosting these courses.

Feedback from participant

I've read to all my children and would like to meet up with others who are keen on it. I moved to Carlisle thirteen years ago and it can be rather isolating to leave your old circle of friends.

The courses have really taken off and we are getting lots of praise from outside the county for what we are doing.
Feedback from Basic Skills Development Worker

Project strengths

· Partnership working
· The outreach workers supplementing work of existing staff.
· Libraries are good venues – they don't have 'school' connotations and have a good set of resources.

Weaknesses

· Geography – Cumbria is a big county to cover and therefore difficult to reach target groups in some places

Tips for other authorities wishing to repeat idea

· Find willing, supportive and proactive partners.
· There needs to be a commitment to put in additional resources to support the project
  e.g. purchasing the right kind of stock.
· Organise staff training and awareness of the project and associated issues
  such as basic skills.
· Ensure that you bid for more than enough funding to carry out
  the project. Remember to put in costs for a project manager
  as well as the workers.
· You definitely need a project manager!

Contact

Sue Cochrane
Business Development
and Marketing Manager

susan.cochrane@cumbriacc.gov.uk
Arroyo Block
The Castle
Carlisle, CA3 8UR
Tel: 01228 607307

The *Touch of...* project

Description of Project

A Touch Of... was the first national reader development project to reach visually impaired readers through an integrated approach involving specialist providers and the public library service. It was made possible by a partnership between National Library for the Blind based in Stockport, the RNIB, Calibre and the Society of Chief Librarians' reader development project *Branching Out*. New resources were created for visually impaired readers to try out a range of reading experiences before deciding which authors to try. From the project ten themed samplers and booklists containing ten titles were created. Each is intended to convey a particular feeling or emotion to the reader and titles overlap many different genres:

A Tender Touch	*A Touch of Tension*
A Velvet Touch	*A Sharp Touch*
A Touch Ticklish	*A Touch of Reality*
A Touch of Terror	*Touching Infinity*
A Healing Touch	*A Touch of Mischief*

Samplers
Each of the booklists has a corresponding sampler with ten extracts from Braille or audio titles available for borrowing from NLB, RNIB and Calibre. There is a reader-friendly introduction to each extract.

Touch of... posters; these can be used in public libraries and in other venues such as community centres, doctors' surgeries and eye clinics. These can be downloaded from the NLB website - www.nlb-online.org

Two more recent NLB projects are:
Make a Noise in Libraries Week (19-25 July 2004)
Aim: to help public libraries to promote their accessible services to visually impaired people as well as encouraging visually impaired people to speak up about their library and information needs.

Read On magazine
A quarterly reading related publication sent to all NLB members. The magazine has the following sections: *News to you*, *Reading matters*, *Reader to reader* (where readers can share information), *Review* (a taste of the more unusual titles added to the library), *Out now* (a selection of titles by favourite authors available at NLB) and *Behind the scenes* (news and features about NLB projects, fundraising and promotions). Recently the magazine has received funding from The Arts Council to provide a section especially for children and young people named *The Book Box*.

Project strengths

· Resources developed for the project are still popular with visually impaired readers long after the launch.

Contact

Linda Corrigan

linda.corrigan@nlbuk.org
National Library for the Blind
Far Cromwell Rd
Bredbury
Stockport
Cheshire SK6 2SG
Tel: 0161 355 2093

Work with Homeless Big Issue vendors

Manchester City Council

At the Big Life Company training centre, Oldham Street, Manchester. 2000 onwards

Description of Project

The project began with informal visits every three to four weeks by a librarian who took in a block loan collection, chatted to vendors about their reading requirements, and took reservations. Out of this grew a poetry writing project.

The project leader set up a regular book club where vendors could share their reading tastes with the group. They looked at genres of fiction such as thrillers and the supernatural, and listened to books on tape. Readings she made from a selection of short stories and poetry proved very popular and were followed by discussions. Two visits by professional storytellers, as well as several visits to Manchester Central Library were organised. At every session there was opportunity for vendors to join the library. Procedures were simplified and vendors without an address could join for a six month period using the Big Life Company address.

Feedback from participants

When's the next Book Club, miss?

The library project has been a definite success story for our vendors and we would like to take this opportunity to thank Maeve and her colleagues for all their hard work and commitment in helping to create better lives for our vendors. **Basic Skills Tutor**

Project strengths

· Satisfying a real need for resources and information on the part of vendors, who are, for the most part, reluctant to enter libraries on their own
· The support of *The Big Issue* staff was invaluable – especially the basic skills tutor.
· The support of the staff in Central Library who showed the vendors round their departments on our visits.

Weaknesses

· Lack of an appropriate venue – we used *The Big Issue* training room, whereas a more informal, comfortable space would have improved the ambience of sessions.
· Difficult to develop the project because of lack of continuity in the vendor clientele attending each session.

Tips for other authorities wishing to repeat idea

· Need to allow enough time for the project to progress steadily and to build up trust with the vendors

Contact

Maeve O'Connor
Co-ordinator Sport and Leisure

moconnor@libraries.manchester.gov.uk
Central Library
St. Peter's Square
Manchester M2 5PD
Tel. 0161 234 1986

88